TOUR CURES

PARTNERS CLUB

GAME IMPROVEMENT LIBRARY™

CREDITS

TOUR CURES

Printed in 2008.

Tom Carpenter
Creative Director

Julie Cisler
Book Design & Production

Michele Stockham
Senior Book Development Coordinator

Steve Hosid
Instruction Editor/Photographer

Steve Ellis
Editor

Ward Clayton   **Leo McCullagh**
John Morris   **Mike Mueller**
PGA TOUR

Special thanks to the following golf courses for allowing us to shoot on location:
Arnold Palmer's Bay Hill Club and Lodge: Orlando, Florida
TPC at River Highlands: Cromwell, Connecticut
The Floridian: Stewart, Florida
Upper Montclair Country Club: Montclair, New Jersey

Acknowledgements
"To the members of the PGA TOUR Partners Club I meet at tournaments around the country: Your questions, comments and support help create articles and books that truly reflect the needs of our outstanding membership."
                                        —*Steve Hosid*

6 7 8 9 / 10 09 08
ISBN 10: 1-58159-130-6
ISBN 13: 978-1-58159-130-9
© 2001 PGA TOUR Partners Club

PGA TOUR Partners Club
12301 Whitewater Drive
Minnetonka, Minnesota 55343
www.partnersclubonline.com

CONTENTS

INTRODUCTION

"Golf is assuredly a mystifying game. It would seem that if a person has hit a golf ball correctly a thousand times, he should be able to duplicate the performance at will. But such is certainly not the case." —Bobby Jones

Let's face it. Golf is a game none of us will ever play perfectly. It's sort of like wrapping a cumbersome present. Just when you think you have it all stuffed perfectly in the package, a part pops out the side. Repackage that part and another one sticks out the bottom. As hard as you try, you can never get all the parts in the package at the same time.

If golf could be easily mastered, it would lose its appeal because, in so many ways, it mirrors life itself. But among us lives a breed of people who must have been blessed by divine intervention. Golf is seemingly easy for them. They live in a world of birdies and, on those occasions when they pass in harm's way, can miraculously extricate themselves triumphantly.

They are professionals, PGA TOUR and SENIOR PGA TOUR professionals, to be specific. What mortal golfers do not see while watching tournament coverage is the thousands of hours of work and practice required to produce the quality of play we all marvel at. What seems second nature to them is a result of continually working on their basics. Those phenomenal recovery shots they come up with under pressure were practiced countless times before.

Just as you have the confidence, knowledge and understanding to handle various situations in your chosen profession, golf's professionals are the experts in their field. Practice and the number of rounds they play keep their skills sharp, and their minds quickly zoom in on the keys needed to master a given shot.

If you're an occasional player, you can't always remember every single nuance of the game. With several days or more between your rounds, little imperfections can creep in and become comfortable, and before you know it another part has popped out of your package.

TOUR Cures will help keep you sharp. Four of golf's top professionals, along with our resident expert, Martin Hall, are on hand to diagnose and correct your problems as they occur. Chi Chi Rodriguez, Fuzzy Zoeller, Bob Murphy and Scott Hoch take on the swing doctor role, providing the same help and encouragement they would if you were to play with them in a PGA TOUR pro-am event.

TOUR Cures pictorially illustrates the problem as well as the cure to quickly help you identify and correct game flaws. I have a chance to meet many Partners Club members during the tournament season and have selected two of them to help show the problems other members have asked for help on.

CASEY CAREY

PATRICK SUGRUE

Casey is a 9-handicap golfer and is the manager of a Prime Equipment rental store. Patrick is an assistant professional at Arnold Palmer's Bay Hill Club and Lodge in Orlando, Florida. Casey worked his way through many of the problems he demonstrates, and Patrick has worked with many golfers to overcome the problems he shows us. Our four professionals and Martin provide the cures.

TOUR Cures is divided into five chapters covering the basics and swing-related problems, specific shots, chipping, putting, and body and equipment problems. Each and every chapter serves as your permanent reference to return you to playing good golf. In *TOUR Cures*, our doctors are always in.

Steve Hosid -Steve Hosid-

ABOUT THE AUTHOR/PHOTOGRAPHER

Steve Hosid is instruction editor, contributing writer and photographer for *PGA TOUR Partners* magazine and the Club's Game Improvement Library. He is co-author of *The Complete Idiot's Guide to Healthy Stretching* (with Chris Verna), and *Golf for Everybody* (with Brad Brewer, former director of The Arnold Palmer Golf Academies), and has collaborated on books with LPGA star Michelle McGann and tennis player MaliVai Washington.

Partners Club President Tom Lehman with Steve Hosid.

Steve is a graduate of the University of Southern California. He and his wife, Jill, live with two non-golfing Borzoi Wolfhounds on the 13th hole at Arnold Palmer's Bay Hill Club in Orlando, Florida.

MEET THE PLAYERS

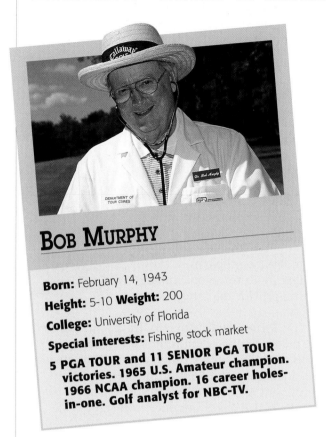

BOB MURPHY

Born: February 14, 1943

Height: 5-10 **Weight:** 200

College: University of Florida

Special interests: Fishing, stock market

5 PGA TOUR and 11 SENIOR PGA TOUR victories. 1965 U.S. Amateur champion. 1966 NCAA champion. 16 career holes-in-one. Golf analyst for NBC-TV.

FUZZY ZOELLER

Born: November 11, 1951

Height: 5-10 **Weight:** 190

Special interests: Fishing, hunting, golf course design

10 PGA TOUR victories, including 1979 Masters and 1984 U.S. Open.

A baseball injury at the University of Florida led to my playing competitive golf. My dad was a scratch player and with Conrad Rehling, my college coach, they helped my game immeasurably.

Wins in the 1965 Florida State Amateur, the U.S. Amateur and the NCAA Championship were the catalyst for thinking about playing golf professionally. A friend, who hired me after college to mostly play golf with his customers, staked me to $20,000 and a car after I told him how afraid I was to wake up one day at age 40 and regret not having tried to play the PGA TOUR.

I began at Pebble Beach and finished second in the Westchester Classic before winning the next two tournaments I played. I've had an even better career on the SENIOR PGA TOUR for a number of reasons, but mainly since getting my transitory arthritis under control. You don't realize how much you miss something until you can't do it anymore.

I remember saying that if the good Lord gives me my hands back, I will be playing the SENIOR TOUR. I enjoy doing television, but not nearly as much as I enjoy competing.

—Bob Murphy

I grew up on a golf course and took the game seriously. One night, along with a buddy, we pried every bit of crabgrass out of a green with our screwdrivers.

The next morning the head pro was standing at my parents' front door. "Where's he at!" he asked lividly. When my parents came to get me out of the bed I had just crawled into, my dad asked, "Son, where were you last night?" My only answer was to tell him I was going to fix that green one day. The green eventually turned out to be the best darn green on the course.

I never really took lessons, and my learning experience was more tips than anything. This taught me to learn by feel, rather than mechanics. I teach my own kids that way, allowing them to develop their own swing before we work on trying a few things.

This is a lot better than trying to find a picture-perfect swing that works all the time. This is how I will help you in *TOUR Cures.*

—Fuzzy Zoeller

CHI CHI RODRIGUEZ

Born: October 23, 1935
Height: 5-7 **Weight:** 132
Special interests: Working with children
8 PGA TOUR and 22 SENIOR PGA TOUR victories.

SCOTT HOCH

Born: November 24, 1955
Height: 5-11 **Weight:** 170
College: Wake Forest University
Special interests: All sports and economics
8 PGA TOUR victories. Won 1996 Vardon Trophy for lowest scoring average.

I took up golf at age seven and worked for 10 cents a round as an apprentice forecaddie. When I became a caddie two years later, my wages increased to 25 cents a round. I left to enter the army at 19, but by that time I had organized the rest of the caddies and our pay had increased to $1.70.

My first lesson was at age 22 when Pete Cooper, the best golfer in Florida, helped me. I had a lot of talent, but a very bad grip. This is where I improved most from Pete. There is no secret to golf; follow the five fundamentals—good grip, good posture, ball position, take-away and follow-through—and you will improve.

My sword dance changed from the first little bit of entertainment I brought to the TOUR. When I started, I used to put my hat over the hole, but a few players claimed I was damaging the hole. The great players at the time never complained, but I decided to change.

I figured the hole was the bull and my putter was the sword, so after a birdie or a great putt I stabbed the bull, dried the blood off my sword and put it back in the scabbard. My mother and father always tried to make people laugh. The good thing is the fans laugh with me, not at me.

—Chi Chi Rodriguez

I began playing golf at age seven. Since everyone in my family played, I picked up my technique from them. With all the great young players in the area, the competition was outstanding. My high school team never lost a match.

Wake Forest University was the defending national champion the year I joined a team that featured Curtis Strange and Jay Haas. I never had a flashy game, but just like now, it was consistent. My first PGA TOUR victory came in my rookie season at Quad Cities.

As the Bob Hope Chrysler Classic defending champion the year three Presidents participated in the pro-am, we all played together along with Mr. Hope. They could have named that round after the movie "The Longest Day!" President Bush played quickly. President Ford would have been a great baseball player because he hit to every field. President Clinton could not take his usual mulligan on every shot, which threw him off his game.

—Scott Hoch

MARTIN HALL

Martin Hall, one of the game's top instructors, provides his proven practice drills throughout this book. Hall appears regularly on the PGA TOUR Partners Video Series and has been selected as one of the 50 best golf instructors in the U.S.

1 DIAGNOSIS AND REFERRAL

Any time you seek professional help, it's wise to provide the expert with as much relevant information about your condition as possible. The sooner a problem can be diagnosed, the sooner the cure can begin.

With many ailments, the symptoms sometimes mask the actual problem. A good medical diagnostician begins each examination with the basics—blood pressure, pulse and some questions to help pinpoint the underlying cause of your problem.

In this opening chapter, some of the most respected players in the game begin by asking the questions, then referring you to the specific *TOUR Cures* areas to help start your game on the road to recovery. There is never any waiting in *TOUR Cures*. The doctors will see you now!

PRO:
BOB MURPHY

QUESTION: FIRST AND FOREMOST, WHERE DOES YOUR BALL GO AFTER YOU HIT IT?

REFERRAL:

Balls that slice or hook are the visual symptoms of the most curable problem of all: improper fundamentals. I know that therapeutic work on your grip, posture, width of stance and ball position may sound like the equivalent of "take two aspirins and call me in the morning," but slicing and hooking usually begin at address.

My recommendation is that before seeking a fancy solution for ball flight problems, join me in Chapter 2 for a full review of a good address position. On the Practice Tee, specialist Martin Hall will also suggest some drills to help resuscitate your game.

If all else fails, Chapter 3 offers some intensive tips. They may not be permanent cures, but trying some may offer temporary relief and allow you to enjoy your game.

— *MURPH*

PRO:
CHI CHI RODRIGUEZ

QUESTIONS: HOW'S YOUR BUNKER PLAY? DO YOU HAVE DIFFICULTY GETTING OUT OF SAND OR CONTROLLING DISTANCE?

REFERRAL:

Ben Hogan called me the "best bunker player he ever saw," so I'll be your sand specialist. Often the cause of poor bunker play is as simple as not understanding how the club should work in the sand. I'll show you some bunker remedies in Chapter 4.

Bunker play does not have to be feared. In fact, in certain situations we pros may actually prefer to hit a shot out of a bunker instead of another landing area. It's easy to spin the ball out of sand, and I'll share my knowledge of this with you.

— *CHI CHI*

PRO: FUZZY ZOELLER

QUESTIONS: DO YOU WASTE STROKES WHEN CHIPPING? DOES THE BALL GO WHERE YOU WANT, OR DO YOU SCUFF THE GROUND OR BLADE IT ACROSS THE GREEN?

REFERRAL:

A good golfer quickly discovers the benefit of chipping the ball close—it eliminates headaches caused by missed approach shots. Good chipping can save you strokes; bad chipping adds needless strokes to your total. I will help you avoid the latter.

You will find my help in Chapter 4, coupled with some excellent drills by the Partners Club Game Improvement Series resident specialist, Martin Hall. Together we will get you on the road to chipping recovery.

A strong chipping game will automatically make you a better putter. It doesn't take a doctorate degree to realize that a short putt is easier to make than a long one.

— *FUZZY*

PRO: SCOTT HOCH

QUESTION: WHEN YOU HAVE TO HIT A SHOT OUT OF THE ROUGH, DO YOU EXPERIENCE DIRECTIONAL OR LENGTH IRREGULARITIES?

REFERRAL:

There are specific cures to fix your rough problems. They require adaptations from normal procedures. I'll help you in Chapter 3.

To be consistent out of the rough, you need to understand the effects of the grass between your clubface and the ball. I'll take the guesswork out of the equation, allowing you to become a better player when in the tall or wiry stuff.

Of course, the best remedy is not to land in the rough. This requires precision off the tee. In Chapter 2, on Martin Hall's Practice Tee, you will find some outstanding drills to help keep your ball flight on line.

— *SCOTT*

PRO: CHI CHI RODRIGUEZ

QUESTIONS: DO YOU SUFFER FROM POOR TARGET SELECTION WHEN PITCHING? DOES YOUR BALL STOP WAY SHORT OR ROLL THROUGH THE GREEN?

REFERRAL:

Nothing is more frustrating than wasting strokes from the shorter distances, so in Chapter 4, I open my bag of cures to help solve your pitching problems. I'll show you how to turn an erratic pitching game into a consistent one that delivers your ball closer to the pin.

Chapter 3 features some of my adaptations for dealing with terrain problems that can affect both pitching distance and accuracy. Accuracy becomes even more important the closer you get to the pin, so if you want to improve quickly I also suggest reviewing some of Martin Hall's swing plane drills in Chapter 2.

— *CHI CHI*

PRO: FUZZY ZOELLER

QUESTION: ARE YOU A GOOD PUTTER?

REFERRAL:

The average putts-per-round for the PGA TOUR is 1.78. The statistical leader averages 1.71. We're always working on our putting to maintain the stroke. Putting must also hold up under the pressure of tournament play.

In Chapter 4, I utilize a unique training aid to show the results of incorrect inside-out or outside-in strokes. The "putterball" also helps me show you how to correct some putting problems that can both frustrate you and cause you higher scores.

Martin Hall has a different approach using a coin. On the Practice Tee at the end of Chapter 4, he works on smoothness and tempo. Incorporating both of those into your stroke will lower your putts-per-round immediately.

— *FUZZY*

Pro:
Bob Murphy

Question: Is Your Body Ready to Make a Good Golf Swing, or Do Inflexibility Compensations Creep In?

Referral:

I'm still in the hunt for victories every week I play. To help keep a professional's body fit and ready on both the PGA TOUR and the SENIOR PGA TOURS, the Health-South fitness trailer accompanies us to every stop. Ralph Simpson is one of the specialists who helps the players fine-tune their bodies for the rigors of competitive golf.

In Chapter 5 Ralph demonstrates some stretches to help free up your body turn. A repeatable swing is the goal of highly skilled golfers, and having a flexible body helps attain that goal. You want to face the target at the finish of a properly struck, on-line golf shot, but it takes flexibility for that to occur.

— *Murph*

Pro:
Scott Hoch

Questions: Does Your Equipment Need a Cure of Its Own? Could Your Shafts Be Creating a Problem? Should Your Putterhead Be Toe, Heel or Center Weighted?

Referral:

Even a perfect swing can bring mixed results if your equipment is not matched to your game. In Chapter 5 we offer some cures for equipment woes.

If you have a favorite club that you always feel confident with and a few others that never feel just right, the problem may be with how the shafts are inserted into the clubhead. We take you into one of the tournament equipment trailers to explain the cure.

Some putters are toe weighted while others are center weighted. Both are designed to provide the type of feel needed to match certain techniques. Chapter 5 will show if your technique matches your putter weighting.

— *Scott*

2

SWING CURES

"Why don't you just aim more to the right?" —*Ben Hogan's answer to an amateur partner when asked for advice on correcting his shots to the left.*

While the cure-all to swing-related problems might not be as simple as Ben Hogan's response above, his statement does underscore the need to give basic fundamentals a periodic checkup. All golfers—including our skilled professionals—are not immune to slipping into occasional bad habits.

In this chapter you will find the pertinent information needed for a major swing reconstruction or merely a slight tweaking. Each of the four sections deals with specific areas to make the ease of your recovery quick and painless.

"You have a lot of checkpoints, but most importantly the club must fit on the ground in a square position." —*Bob Murphy*

IN THIS SECTION

ADDRESS

- Grip

- Grip Pressure

- Posture

- Alignment

- Square Clubhead

- Ball Position

- Stance

- Eliminate Tension

- Practice Tee

TAKE-AWAY AND BACKSWING

- Correct Swing Image

- Swinging, Not Picking

- Correct Backswing Track

- Swing Plane

- Coordinated Body Turn

- Correct Hip Position

- Correct Weight Transfer

- Swing Tempo

- Practice Tee

TOP OF THE SWING

- Correct Swing Plane

- Timing

- Tempo

- Correct Transition

- Practice Tee

DOWNSWING TO FOLLOW-THROUGH

- Maintaining Linkage

- Proper Release

- Keeping the Power

- Follow-Through for Power and Accuracy

- Practice Tee

ADDRESS

Golf is an athletic sport that requires an athletic address. The accuracy and consistency golfers strive for can be found within the five basic fundamentals of a good swing. Four of them—grip, posture, head position and ball position—occur as you address the ball. The $64,000 question is: Do you set up correctly every time?

Even if you have a finely tuned swing, this section is a good reference tool. Regardless of your skill level, the simplest of bad habits can creep into your swing and become comfortable. Once that occurs, compensations take root that eventually wreak havoc on your swing.

Incorrect hand or ball positions at address require your brain to make swing adjustments to get the club back to the ball. The cure is pretty simple, as Bob Murphy demonstrates. Martin Hall's drills at the end of the chapter ensure your continued health at address.

PROBLEM 1
GRIP: INCORRECT HAND POSITIONS

SYMPTOM

Check your glove for this symptom. Holding the club too much in the palm of your left hand (right hand for left-handed players) causes the palm to wear out or tear.

Gripping the club incorrectly (above photos) in the fingers or across the palm of your left hand prevents your hands from working together during the swing. Accuracy and distance are adversely affected because the hands can't square the clubface at impact, and your wrists can't hinge and unhinge naturally as you swing.

Another visible grip problem occurs when the fingers are closed around the shaft. The V's formed between the thumb and forefingers of both hands are the indicators. Grips that are too strong often create severe hooking, and feature the V's (left photo) pointing incorrectly outside the right shoulder.

The V's in the right photo incorrectly point to the left shoulder. This is a weak grip and brings an open clubface back to the ball, causing a slice.

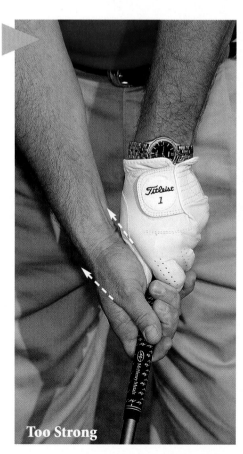

Too Strong

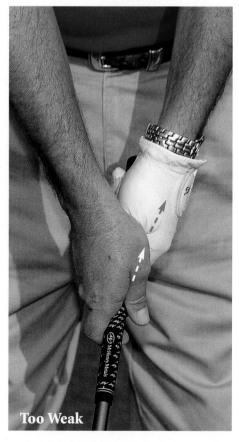

Too Weak

TOUR CURE 1-A
CORRECT LEFT HAND GRIP

Gripping the club correctly promotes the free-flowing swing needed to produce distance and accuracy. Once properly positioned, the hands can work harmoniously together, freeing your wrists to hinge and unhinge naturally. As the clubhead is swung down, it can arrive square to the target line at impact.

We will devote several pages of this book to show how a club must be gripped correctly. The grip is *that* important to shot-making success!

The blue lines on my glove show where I want the left hand positioned on the club, compared to the incorrect location across the fingers. Holding it too much in the fingers contributes to the lack of grip firmness I see with many amateurs.

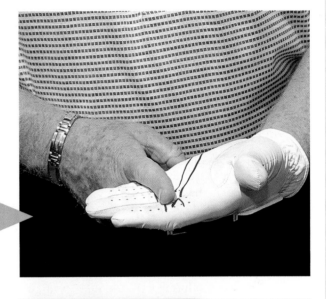

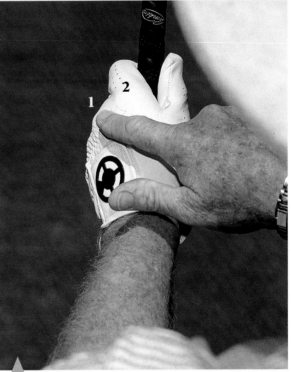

Lay the club diagonally across the base of the left fingers and across the palm. Be sure to allow the butt of the club to extend past your left hand about a half-inch. Compare this with the incorrect grip as shown by the red lines.

As you hold the club in front of you, two prominent knuckles on the left hand should be visible (numbered 1 and 2 above). If you see three knuckles, the left hand is too strong, while one knuckle indicates the grip is too weak. For most players, the thumb should be on the right side of the shaft, as shown.

TOUR CURE 1-B
CORRECT RIGHT HAND GRIP

The right hand should hold the club mostly in the fingers. This significantly increases your sense of feel and promotes a harmonious working relationship with your left hand.

We will deal with grip pressure, but for now just place the right hand correctly on the club. Scott Hoch will demonstrate two methods to customize your grip for your personal preference.

Look at the blue line drawn down the lifeline of my right hand. The lifeline should be over the left hand's thumb when the grip closes.

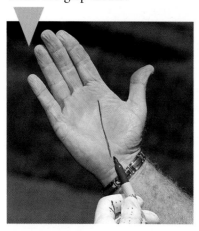

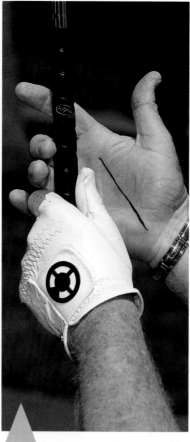

Grip the club with the right hand at the base of the fingers where they meet the palm. Do not grab the club tightly. Gently ease into the position to encourage a tension-free grip.

With the grip closed and the club held out in front of you, only two knuckles on the left hand (1 and 2, below) should be visible. The right hand thumb and forefinger knuckle should also be seen.

SCOTT'S GRIP ADAPTATIONS

Here are two ways to customize your grip for your personal preference. After positioning the club as Murph demonstrated above, you can either overlap or interlock your grip.

Both Bob and I prefer the overlap grip, which places the pinkie of the right hand into the groove between the second and third fingers of the left hand. Some golfers prefer to interlock the right-hand pinkie with the left hand's second finger. Jack Nicklaus prefers this method. Try both and compare the results.

OVERLAP GRIP

INTERLOCK GRIP

TOUR CURE 1-C
GRIP CHECK

A correct grip encourages swinging the club on the proper path. The best way to check if you have gripped the club correctly is to check the position of the V's formed between the thumb and forefingers of both hands.

Earlier, we showed the incorrect V positions and discussed the problems they cause (see page 18). The key here is to check that your V's are not too strong or too weak.

The V's should point between your chin and right shoulder for right-handed golfers (below), or inside the chin and left shoulder for left-handed golfers. As your skill level increases, adjust the V's slightly weaker or stronger depending on the shape of the shot you want to hit.

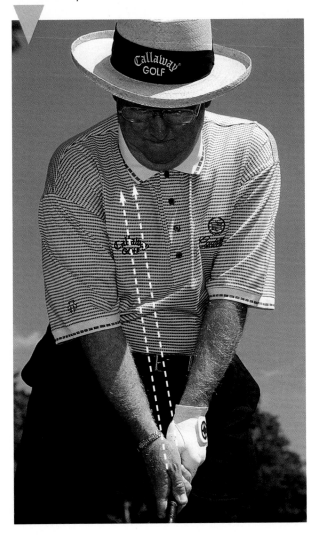

BOB'S GRIP TIPS

• One size does not fit all, so be sure the grip on your club fits your hands. A correctly fitting grip allows the fingers of your left hand to wrap around the club and gently press into your palm.

• Practice your grip at home to make it feel natural.

• Use a commercially available short club or cut one down so you can develop an awareness of the grip in relation to the position of the clubhead.

PROBLEM 2
LOSING GRIP DURING SWING

TOUR CURE 2
CORRECT GRIP PRESSURE

Losing the grip during your swing is a problem that normally occurs at the top of the backswing. The butt of the club separates from the fleshy part of your left hand. Hitting the ball on the toe—a problem we cure in Chapter 3—causes you to lose your grip at impact.

Re-gripping in mid-swing leads to a variety of outcomes, but doesn't lead to good scoring. As you re-grip, the relationship between your grip and clubhead slightly changes and the clubhead can vary several degrees from being square at impact.

My grip pressure at address is on the last three fingers of the left hand. The pressure is nice and firm. I keep the right hand relaxed. As you get to the top of the backswing, the right hand naturally gains slight pressure to hold on to the club on the way down.

If you begin with a lot of right-hand pressure, you will lose it on the way back and then have to re-grip the club on the way to the ball. To develop the correct feeling, try this tip I learned from Jim Flick and Jack Nicklaus.

GRIP PRESSURE CHECK

Hold the club in front of you about waist high (1) and then let it drop down to a horizontal position (2). The pressure needed to hold it waist high is all the grip pressure you need at address. Pressure will be noticeable in only the last three fingers of the left hand (red fingers, 3). Your right hand should feel free of pressure.

Losing grip during swing.

As he reaches the top of his backswing, Murph exerts just enough grip pressure to keep his club positioned properly. Too much pressure tightens the muscles and restricts the swing.

PROBLEM 3
POOR ADDRESS POSTURE

Casey is demonstrating two examples of poor address. While different in appearance, they share a common flaw: They destroy your swing before you've swung!

SPINE ANGLE TOO BENT OVER

SPINE ANGLE TOO UPRIGHT

Golf is an athletic sport that requires athletic motions. Regardless of your age, body type or skill level, you must create both balance and body flex in your address posture.

With positions like those shown here—it's virtually impossible to build a repeatable golf swing. Without a flexed and balanced address posture as its foundation, the swing will come crashing down.

TOUR CURE 3
ESTABLISHING GOOD BODY POSTURE

Here is a good way to arrive at a perfectly flexed and balanced posture at address. I'm standing on a bench, ready to jump. If we jumped together, we wouldn't land on our heels or flat on our feet because we would land out of balance. We would land toward the balls of our feet, and our knees would be flexed to absorb the force of the landing. Landing stiff-legged would hurt.

Our upper body would also land as straight up as possible, because a forward or backward lean would be off balance, causing a fall. Our bottoms would be sticking out, setting an athletic spine angle. The slight upper body tilt is totally in balance, and the arms hang down naturally.

Put a golf club in our hands and we are ready to go, because this is what I call a good athletic address posture position.

PROBLEM 4
POOR BODY ALIGNMENT AT ADDRESS

SLICING MISALIGNMENT

Slicing misalignment—front foot back.

HOOKING MISALIGNMENT

Hooking misalignment—rear foot back.

Golf is a target sport. However, unlike aiming down a rifle barrel or drawing a bow and looking down the arrow, golfers must stand to the side of the target line to aim. It's common for golfers of all skill levels to encounter occasional alignment problems, preventing them from achieving optimum accuracy.

Compounding the problem is our rotational golf swing. Ideally, we should have various parts of our body parallel to the target line. If our shoulders or feet are not aligned parallel, and we attempt to swing down the target line, other problems arise, most notably slicing and hooking.

Trying to aim the clubface more in one direction to compensate only makes matters worse. The two photos above show examples of incorrect body-to-target alignment.

TOUR CURE 4
CORRECT ALIGNMENT

Even with a wide-open fairway ahead, professionals always have a target as their aiming point. Various parts of your body need to be set up parallel to the target line.

Attend any PGA TOUR or SENIOR PGA TOUR event and watch us practice on the range. Notice how we put clubs down on the ground to work on alignment. Let's do the same thing here.

1 - PARALLEL CLUBS

Place two clubs parallel on the ground with your ball between them. Stand with your toes touching the inside club.

2 - SHOULDERS, KNEES AND HIPS

We already know the feet are parallel to the target line. The shoulders, hips and knees must also be parallel. Check this by holding a club in front of you. The club should look parallel to the other clubs as you look down.

3 - DROP INTO POSITION

Confident that you are properly aligned to the target, drop down to a flexed, balanced, athletic position.

PROBLEM 5
ACCIDENTAL MISALIGNMENT

Even if your setup is parallel to the target line, another problem can creep in.

As you took one final look at your target, how did you move your head? If you raised up and rotated your body, you changed your parallel shoulder position—and probably your knees—to be open to the target line. Frustrated golfers trying to cure a slice may have overlooked this seemingly benign problem.

Raising up and turning your head can also unknowingly change other previously parallel to the target line body positions. This inadvertent misalignment may be the cause of your slicing.

TOUR CURE 5
ROTATE YOUR CHIN UP

The key to correcting inadvertent shoulder misalignment is to know how to correctly move your head to look at the target. Instead of lifting the head and turning it, try to rotate your chin up.

As you rotate the chin, the shoulders and knees are not required to make any movement and will remain parallel to the target line. Guard against even the slightest movement that can take you out of your parallel position.

PROBLEM 6
CLUB INCORRECTLY ALIGNED TO THE BALL

Your club is designed to sit squarely on the ground. If you take a parallel stance and the clubhead is incorrectly aligned to your target, the toe or heel comes off the ground, as the photos below show.

Misdirected shots are the only possible outcome. Even a few degrees off has an adverse effect, tempting you to mistakenly adjust your body alignment to compensate on the next shot. Unfortunately, this tends to make things even worse.

AIMED LEFT/HEEL UP

AIMED RIGHT/TOE UP

TOUR CURE 6
SQUARE CLUBHEAD

As part of any good pre-shot routine, good players start their address by placing the club behind the ball. Next, they walk in, do some adjusting and take their grip, knowing the club is properly aimed at the target.

They are secure in knowing that if they set up parallel, the club will also be on line. A clubhead on line is also a clubhead that is squarely touching the ground.

I've placed a black cloth under my clubhead to illustrate what a square position should look like. You can have a lot of checkpoints in a golf swing, but most importantly the club must fit on the ground in a square position.

BOB'S EQUIPMENT TIPS

Be sure the *lower portion* of the club is square to your target line. Some members make the mistake of aligning the top of the club to the ball.

To make aiming easier, manufacturers provide unique aids on the clubface, as shown below. When you shop for equipment, always take this type of user-friendly engineering into consideration.

PROBLEM 7
DOOMED-TO-FAIL BALL POSITION

Most golfers with this problem don't understand that the ball should usually be positioned at the bottom of their swing arc. This is the only position where the clubhead can impact it square to the target line.

If the ball is too far forward in the stance, the clubface will be closed at impact. If the ball is too far back, the clubface will be open. Unless you are deliberately trying to shape a shot, these positions will result in inconsistent ball flights, or thin and chunked shots. If you tend to spray your shots, this may be the cause.

FORWARD IN STANCE   *BACK IN STANCE*

With the ball too far forward in the stance, the clubface will be closed at impact.   *With the ball too far back in the stance, the clubface will be open at impact.*

TOUR CURE 7
BOTTOM OF SWING ARC BALL POSITION

The cure for establishing correct ball position is similar to our last cure, because the clubface must be square on the ground. When I make a swing, my hand and impact positions must be aligned.

Set up to the ball correctly and you should be able to draw a straight line down your left arm through the shaft. The ball will then be positioned correctly and the bottom edge of the club will be squarely on the ground.

PROBLEM 8
WIDTH OF STANCE

STANCE TOO WIDE

Consistency is the foundation of good golf, but all too often amateurs fail to understand the importance of setting up to the ball the same way every time. While those of us on the TOUR have developed pre-shot routines that help us consistently duplicate our positions, most amateurs just take a couple of practice swings and casually step in.

The most common mistake is taking too wide of a stance, thinking it creates balance and power. Power in golf is derived from the smooth transfer of weight back and through the ball. A wide stance makes this difficult.

You want to coil up over your back leg. With a wide stance (above left), notice how far you have to sway (above right) to get over to that leg. Now shorten your stance to shoulder-width distance and try it again. You can feel the weight transfer over smoothly. Having a stance that is too wide inhibits hip rotation.

TOUR CURE 8
PRE-SHOT ROUTINE

Consistency is built on familiarity. The margin of error decreases the more you do something the same way every time. While watching tournaments, you see the pros go through the same pre-shot motions every time they address the ball.

Individuality is important, because what works for Tiger Woods is different from what works for me or you. As you develop a pre-shot routine, create a method that assures a similar width of stance for each shot, and adjust the width depending on the club.

MURPH'S PRE-SHOT ROUTINE

I come into the shot from behind, keeping an open body to the target and my right hand on the club. I put the club squarely on the ground behind the ball.

I grip the club with two hands and then start to adjust the width of my stance. Ball position varies, depending on the length of the club.

The width of my stance is my own personal preference, based on what practice and experience has shown works best for me. A good starting point is to have your feet shoulder-width apart. Use your pre-shot routine for every shot you hit on the course and on the range.

PROBLEM 9
FROZEN WITH TENSION

Cobwebs won't form around you, as we jokingly show in our photograph of a golfer frozen with tension. But the point should be well taken. Some members may actually freeze over the ball, and this inactivity causes them to tighten up.

Instead of a free-flowing, efficient swing, tension produces a stiff, herky-jerky effort. Dust off those cobwebs and let me help you rid yourself of muscle-paralyzing tension.

TOUR CURE 9
CREATE MOTION

I have two cures to eliminate tension from your address position. The first is to have confidence that you have set yourself up to the ball correctly—with a good grip, proper alignment and posture—and the ball is positioned properly. Now is the time to set the trigger and create some motion.

MURPH'S FORWARD PRESS

As you work on your pre-shot routine, include something that begins the motion. Gary Player tucks his right knee in. I use a slight forward press that sets up the angle on the back of my left hand. It takes motion to do this, and it avoids the temptation to delay the start.

LEFT HAND ANGLE

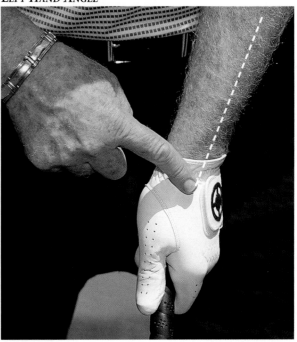

PRACTICE TEE

Here are some additional drills and suggestions that will help you put into practice the cures Bob Murphy gave you. The grip is your lifeline to the club.

All good instruction should start by making sure that your hands establish a good working relationship.

GRIP HELPER

These two suggestions make it easier to grip the club properly. Either take the grip with your left arm hanging by your side (near-right photo), or with the shaft eye level in front of you (far-right photo).

ELBOW/GRIP PRESSURE DRILL

You don't want a death grip on the club. Tight grips create tight muscles which inhibit the free-flowing swing you need. Since more people err on the side of gripping the club too tightly, this tip should help:

Unlock your elbows! It's very rare that people will hold the club too tightly if they have relaxed elbow joints.

If you are holding the club too tightly, your arms and elbows are locked. If that is your problem, begin by taking your normal grip.

Moving your elbows up and then returning them to the previous position will keep your grip free of tension.

KEEP THE TEES DRILL

If you are losing your grip at impact, you are hitting the ball with the club's toe. We will help you in Chapter 3. If you are losing your grip during the swing, incorporate Bob Murphy's cure with this simple test. It helps you understand the difference between having a desirable light grip or an undesirable loose one.

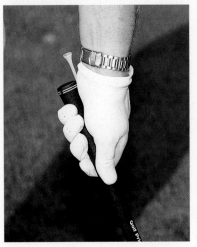

1 Place a tee between the palm of your gloved hand (left for right-handers and right for left-handers) and the grip.

2 As you place your ungloved hand on the club, place a second tee on the palm and close the grip. Using only light grip pressure with the tees in this position, keep the tees in place throughout your swing.

POINT YOUR BELT AT THE BALL

How much should you bend while addressing the ball? If you bend forward too much, your swing will tend to go in-to-out, and you will hit push shots. A posture that is too straight will cause a flat swing. The key that tells you how far forward to bend is your belt buckle. It should point to the ball.

1 Stand tall soldier, pull those shoulder blades together and raise your chin! This is similar to being at attention on the parade ground. Hold your club across your hips.

2 Bend forward at the hips, flexing the knees slightly.

3 Bend forward until your belt buckle points to the ball, as I'm doing with the club (inset). My posture sets up some very good body angles to make an excellent swing.

AIM DOWN THE TARGET LINE

Aiming the clubface is a tendency for some amateurs to compensate for the last shot they hit. Slicers tend to have the clubface too closed at address, while hookers have it too open.

This is a compensation that can work, but if you have changed something in your address position or swing path, you must now aim the club square to the target line. To correct this aiming problem, visualize that you have a short pointer on your clubface. Place a club on the ground or stretch a tight line to simulate a target line.

Visualizing the pointer in your mind, set the club so it points straight down the target line. Condition your mind to this concept and you will be aiming the club more accurately when you play.

BALL POSITION DRILL

The ball should be positioned between the left side of your face and your left shoulder if you are a right-handed golfer; the opposite if you are left-handed. This represents the bottom of the swing arc where the club arrives square to the ball at impact.

To illustrate, I have attached a ruler to a club shaft to provide a better perspective.

PERFECT POSITION

BOTTOM OF ARC

TOO FAR BACK

TOO FAR FORWARD

The crossed lines represent the bottom of the swing arc position. Notice how the ruler is square to the target line and will produce an on-line shot.

If you make a perfect swing but the ball is an inch too far back, the club will be open at impact. For a less-skilled player, the shot will most likely go to the right.

If the ball is too far forward in the stance, the clubface has more time to close at impact. This can cause off-line shots to the left.

As you can see, the bottom of my swing arc is between my face and left shoulder. Using that as a constant, I can position the ball properly every time.

Swing
Cures:
Address

35

ADJUST STANCE AND BALL POSITION FOR DIFFERENT CLUBS DRILL

The ball position and width of your stance will change to accommodate different clubs. To illustrate this, I placed two shoulder-width plastic sticks on the ground along with a dog leash I staked to represent the target line. You can use this practice idea in your backyard and on the practice range.

DRIVER STANCE

6-IRON STANCE

9-IRON STANCE

I take a wider stance to provide a stronger base for a more powerful hit. It also encourages a sweeping approach to the ball. The ball is positioned opposite my left armpit.

I stand with my heels just on the outside of the sticks. The ball is positioned between the left side of my face and my left shoulder to allow more of a downward ball strike.

My stance is on the sticks and the ball is positioned off the left side of my face. I will take a steeper descent for this stroke.

TAKE-AWAY AND BACKSWING

As the club starts back, the first few feet are referred to as the take-away. A more appropriate title would be "the moment of truth."

Coordinating the movement of separate body parts into a smooth, one-piece take-away is the equivalent of a sculptor chiseling away the outer layers of rock until the basic shape of his work becomes visible: One incorrect stroke and the rock shatters. Likewise, the swing will collapse at this early stage with one wrong movement.

Scott Hoch opens this section by curing the wrong idea many golfers have about the shape of the golf swing. Bob Murphy joins in, and together they keep you on the correct path, fixing problems along the way. Martin Hall's Practice Tee drills provide some preventive care to ward off backswing ills.

PROBLEM 10
INCORRECT IMAGE OF A SWING

From some of the swings I see during pro-ams, many of my partners—and probably golfers in general—could improve their games by developing the correct mental image of how a golf swing should look. A golf swing is a journey, and you can either begin on the right road or spend your time zigzagging to your destination.

A major problem can be attributed to the many tips people pick up and misunderstand, like *turn your hips*, *turn your shoulders* and *shift your weight*. From some of the swing positions I've seen, you have to be an extraordinary athlete just to get back to the ball.

Casey is demonstrating one of the variations. Starting from a decent stance (**1**), he starts swinging back, feeling he's doing everything correctly. But he is making a big shoulder turn (**2**), and turning his hips and shifting his weight (**3**). Unfortunately, he's turned on an incorrect shallow-around-the-back swing plane!

TOUR CURE 10
CORRECT BACKSWING IMAGE

The early morning dew coming off my club provides a unique visual to help you understand the correct backswing shape. It goes up *and* around, not just up and not just around.

The water droplets are drawing the curved line of the continuous, smooth movement. When I return to the ball, the club will follow a slightly lower plane. Take some practice swings trying to duplicate the shape of my backswing. Martin Hall has some outstanding drills to help you on the Practice Tee.

PROBLEM 11
PICKING UP THE CLUB

Initiating the golf swing with just the hands leads to a picking-up-the-clubhead movement that immediately destroys all hope for a good swing. *Swing* the club, don't pick it up.

When you pick up the club, the swing starts too vertically. This narrows the swing arc, requiring a steep downward movement back to the ball. This is not desirable.

As you worked diligently on correcting your address position, you also developed and pre-set certain angles, such as the relationship between your spine and lower body. Picking up the club, instead of swinging it back, negates these angles.

Despite a good stance (left), picking up the club (right) negates any possibility of a good swing.

TOUR CURE 11
PUSH LEFT SHOULDER AWAY

Conrad Rehling, my coach at the University of Florida, helped my take-away with this swing thought: There should be a bar attached to your left shoulder that continues down the shaft to the middle of the clubhead.

This welded-together feeling means that to start the swing back, you have to begin by pushing your left shoulder so that everything stays intact. Nothing moves until every-thing moves.

Imagine a bar welded from your left shoulder down the shaft through the middle of the club-head. It all has to move together!

PROBLEM 12
POOR TAKE-AWAY SWING TRACK

The most common mistake as the back-swing begins is taking the clubhead immediately to the inside. This is a great example of a misunderstood golf tip.

Instructors stress the need for an inside-to-square-to-inside swing, but what you may not understand is that this should be a natural result of swinging the club along an arc, instead of trying to help it happen.

The opposite problem is taking the club back straight, which closes the clubface. Here again, a better understanding of the shape of the golf swing can help clear up the problem.

INCORRECT INSIDE PATH

INCORRECT CLOSED FACE TAKE-AWAY

TOUR CURE 12
CORRECT TAKE-AWAY PATH

If you continue using my college coach's steel bar swing tip (previous page), you will always be on the correct path back. Keeping the connected feeling of the shoulders, arms, hands and clubhead intact prevents getting to the inside prematurely.

The following cure will help if your problem is having a swing path too "inside." It also will help those who take the club back too straight and closed.

As you stay connected, swing the club back, trying to keep it as square as possible. The club will begin an arc toward the inside as a result of the natural rotation of your shoulders. Your return to the ball will be on the same arc as your take-away.

Stay connected, keeping your club as square as possible on your take-away.

PROBLEM 13
FLAT OR STEEP SWING

Flat Swing Plane

Tucking the elbow close to the body during the backswing is another example of a frequently misunderstood swing tip. While you do not want the elbow to fly away, some separation from the torso is needed to avoid the flat swing plane we see in the photo below.

The take-away must go both back and up. If you have a video camera, tape your swing and stop the action in this position. You can quickly detect if you have this *flat swing* problem by drawing an imaginary line from the butt of the shaft.

Steep Swing Plane

A steep swing plane is a result of trying not to get into trouble by getting too far away from the target path. Instead of trusting the powers of centrifugal force to swing the clubhead back along the correct arc to impact, you may think brute force and a powerful swing will control it.

If you have a steep swing plane, you must have deep descents. This is the motion it will take to get the club square back to the ball. Instead of a smooth-flowing, effortless swing, it is steep and unproductive. The symptom can be detected by checking the grip of the club.

FLAT SWING PLANE PROBLEM

STEEP SWING PLANE PROBLEM

If the grip of your club points to the ball target line or past it at the halfway point in your backswing (dotted line), your swing plane is too flat.

Your swing plane is too steep if, halfway into your backswing, the grip of your club is pointing to your shoes (arrow).

TOUR CURE 13
USE BOTH ENDS OF THE CLUB

A way to cure your swing plane problems is to use both ends of the club. If you grip the club correctly at address and push the left shoulder back on the take-away, the clubhead should point straight in the air once the shaft reaches horizontal. I'm checking my position in the photo below.

From this horizontal position, all you have to do is swing straight up, as Scott has done below. The line from the grip of his club points downward to just inside the ball, verifying an excellent swing plane. Compare this to the problem photos on the facing page.

TOE POINTS UP

Horizontal club in backswing, clubhead points straight up.

GRIP POINTS INSIDE OF BALL

Top of backswing, grip of club points just inside the ball.

PROBLEM 14
COMPLETING BODY TURN TOO EARLY

TOUR professionals' swings look so effortless because our tempo and timing allow all the moving elements of an efficient golf swing to come together smoothly. But, on occasion, we can suffer from the same malady that less-skilled players struggle with.

Getting out of sync at the start by turning the hips and lower body too early in the backswing causes this problem. If the lower body initiates the backswing, it has less distance to rotate; consequently, your arms and hands can't catch up, and you can't wind up your torso powerfully at the top of your backswing.

A good way to test this problem is to either watch yourself in slow motion on videotape or stop your swing when your hips complete their turn: The key to solving the problem is not to allow the hips to turn all the way back, as my cure shows.

TOUR CURE 14
TURN SHOULDERS, RESIST WITH HIPS

The hips do not turn all the way back. Instead, they are supposed to resist being pulled into the backswing by your shoulder turn. This resistance winds you up like a powerful spring that releases distance-producing energy on your downswing.

Look at my action shots below. I'll point out the relationship between my upper and lower body.

At the top of my backswing, my arms have swung as far as they can go and my back is facing the target. The resistance of my hips has not turned them back as far. The wrinkles in my shirt also show how my body has powerfully coiled like a spring. This is a power position ready to release stored-up energy.

HIPS RESIST UPPER BODY TURN

SCOTT HOCH'S UPPER BODY BEGINS THE TURN

I begin the first three feet of my backswing with my upper body. I do it slowly, which is extremely important to the smoothness of the swing. Notice that I am swinging the clubhead, hands, arms and shoulders back together. You do not see any hip rotation in these two photos. Instead, you see the triangular relationship and the grip of the club staying in front of my body.

Compare the shoulder and hip lines to see how I have turned each during the backswing. You start to see some hip rotation as the big shoulder turn pulls them along, but my hips are offering some resistance.

PROBLEM 15
INCOMPLETE BODY TURN

You may have been told that rushing your swing is responsible for some bad shots. Swinging too fast may be a symptom, but the real problem is making an incomplete backswing.

Your swing needs the time for a lot of moving parts to come together at one vital moment—impact. For that to occur, a certain amount of time has to be allowed for the downswing. A backswing that is too short does not provide enough distance for the downward moving club to travel.

The result is something that looks rushed (as at right).

A short backswing will get you into trouble.

TOUR CURE 15
BACK TO THE TARGET

Your flexibility guides how straight your left arm can be on the backswing and how close you can bring the club to parallel. Although I'm not at parallel in the photos at right, I still completed the backswing, as my back to the target indicates.

If you have followed all of the TOUR Cures in this chapter, this is a natural part of your backswing. Incorporate this concept into your swing—**back to the target on the backswing and face the target at follow-through**. This will go a long way toward improving both the length and effectiveness of your swing.

Remember: Your back faces the target at the top of the backswing, as evidenced in these two views.

PROBLEM 16
INCORRECT WEIGHT TRANSFER

Reverse pivot best describes the condition we see on this page. How your weight is transferred affects the power and ball flight your swing generates.

As we see here, Casey has made a full turn but unfortunately left something behind—his weight. If, on the backswing, your weight remains on the side of your body that is closest to the target, you made a reverse pivot.

The problem continues on your downswing. As you swing back to the ball, the weight will incorrectly transfer to the side of your body farthest from the target. Weight fuels swing power, so if you reverse pivot you are running on empty.

TOUR CURE 16
LOAD UP ON THE RIGHT SIDE

As you look at the large photo of my backswing, notice how my left heel has lifted. If the weight had incorrectly stayed on that side of my body, lifting the heel would be impossible.

My weight has transferred over to the right side of my body and is over the right leg; I can feel it on the inside of my right foot. My swing is fully fueled, so when I transition into the downswing, I have all of this energy to transfer forward toward the ball. This means power and distance.

At the top of Murph's backswing (inset), notice how he coils over his right leg. As he swings back, the weight smoothly transfers over and he feels it in the instep of his right foot. Practicing at home in front of a mirror allows you to see and feel your weight transferring correctly.

PROBLEM 17
ROCKET BACKSWING

You don't hit the ball on your backswing, so don't rocket back! The quicker you understand that, the better off you will be. The complete amount of time a golf swing takes is a second and a half. The backswing takes a full second, and the downswing to follow-through takes a half-second.

This rocket-propelled backswing is fast at the wrong time. The clubhead needs to move at the highest rate of speed through impact. It should not attempt to escape the earth's atmosphere while trying to reach the top of the backswing! If so, your tempo and timing is thrown off. This is one mission that should be scrubbed before it takes off.

TOUR CURE 17
THINK POSITION AT THE TOP

The cure for slowing down your backswing is to think more about placing the club into a position from which you can then go forward. It's important to get to the top correctly. This is how I developed my famous pause.

I want to get to the top as smoothly as possible and be ready to begin my downswing in full control. Each of us has a different internal tempo. Scott Hoch swings back faster than I do, but he is still completely under control. Scott also firmly believes that the first few feet of his swing must begin slowly.

FINDING THE PROPER POSITIONS

As I swing back under control, my connected take-away (1) begins the club on the correct inside track (2). The toe is correctly pointing up (3) and the grip of the club points inside the ball (4). I finish my backswing in the perfect coiled position, with my back toward the target (5).

PRACTICE TEE

I like to use this monstrous plane board as a reference to help you with your swing. Before we start with the take-away, I believe you will benefit most by creating an image in your mind of how the swing should look. The swing is circular and follows an inclined plane.

CORRECT BACKSWING IMAGE

As you look at the board, the most relevant portion is from hip high to hip high. This is the only time during the swing that the shaft will touch the board.

On the backswing, the left elbow stays on the same plane above hip height, but the shaft goes up. On the follow-through after hip height, the right elbow stays on the plane as the shaft goes up and around.

PLANE PROBLEMS

TOO INSIDE

Taking the club back too inside drops it below the swing plane.

TOO STEEP

Trying to keep the clubhead square on take-away leads to this incorrect position, outside of the plane.

BRUSH DRILL

Harvey Penick used this drill to help his students develop the feel of brushing away from the ball, instead of picking up the club. He used a garden-variety weed cutter and had them brush it back and forth as if they were cutting away the weeds. It works!

RAISED-HEEL DRILL

To avoid turning your body too early in the backswing, try raising your right heel at address. Don't put it back down until you have swung back to the hip-high position. You simply can't turn inside prematurely with a raised heel.

HIP TURN DRILL

You should *turn* in your swing, not slide. Try this drill to help you develop that feeling. It begins by placing a club across your thighs (left).

Maintain a little bit of pressure as you turn the club back and forth on your thighs (left). Keep the club level as you turn, and the position will duplicate how your hips and thighs should look and feel during the swing (right).

Swing
Cures:
Take-Away
and
Backswing

SHOULDER TURN DRILL

This practice drill develops the feeling for how much shoulder turn is needed in your swing. All you need is a club and a stick.

Begin by placing a stick (or another club) on the ground on the inside of your right heel. Cross your arms as you put a club across your shoulders.

Turn the club until it's parallel to the stick by your foot. This photo also shows the club on my shoulders is past the parallel stick on the ground. Proper weight shifting happens because I've coiled over my right leg.

BALL UNDER RIGHT FOOT DRILL

Bob and Scott want you to feel the weight on the inside of your right foot as you turn during the backswing. By putting a ball under the outside of your right foot as you turn, you will effortlessly be able to begin developing this feeling.

If you have a problem sliding or swaying during your backswing, this will help prevent it. You will feel the right knee staying inside of the right foot.

CORRECT WEIGHT CHECK DRILL

The problem of reverse pivoting can be eliminated once you develop the feel of proper weighting. If you have transferred the weight to the right side on your backswing, check yourself by lifting your left foot (below left).

Correctly transferring the weight forward to your left side during your downswing allows you to lift your right foot after your follow-through (below right). If you are still reverse pivoting, you will not be able to lift the appropriate foot.

PUSH BACK DRILL

A good cure for a fast backswing is to place another ball behind your clubface (below left). As you swing back, see how short of a distance you can roll the second ball back. If you are too quick, the ball will go flying back, instead of a short roll away (below right).

TOP OF THE SWING

Coming from a baseball background, Bob Murphy's golf swing early on was aggressive. And, as he says, "Aggressive translates into quick, which translates into rapid, which translates into out of control." The cure to his problem: converting the top of his backswing into one very quiet moment.

Bob's solution was to swing to the top, pause significantly and then start down to the ball. Going to that extreme may not be necessary for you, but it does point out the vital need to establish a smooth transition from the backswing to the downswing.

With Murph's help and Martin Hall's Practice Tee drills, the top of your backswing can be taken off the sick list.

PROBLEM 18
TOO UPRIGHT OR TOO FLAT

An incorrect posture at address has created the top of the backswing problems seen here at this critical phase of the swing. While other problems sometimes may be responsible, the blame most likely can be traced to the cause-and-effect theory.

Being too bent over at address causes the backswing to be too upright at the top. And standing too tall at address leads to a flat swing plane at the top. Understanding the basic relationship of angles provides clues as to how important it is to set the correct posture angle at address.

TIPPED OVER=BACKSWING TOO UPRIGHT

TOO TALL=BACKSWING TOO FLAT

- Bent over too much at the waist.

- Trying to maintain balance, the left arm must rise off the chest and follow the steep angle set at address going back.

- Top of the backswing becomes too upright (inset photo).

- Downswing will be overly steep.

- Deep divots, fat or skied shots, and slices are symptoms.

- Standing too tall.

- Angle will only allow the shoulders to turn on a flat plane.

- Shallow swing path back to ball (inset photo).

- Loss of power, hitting behind the ball, and topped shots are symptoms.

TOUR CURE 18
SET ANGLE AND ROTATE SHOULDERS

Setting the correct spine angle at address is mandatory if you want to arrive at the top correctly. This angle is determined by how much you bend forward at the hips. The Practice Tee drill in Chapter 2 helps you consistently set the correct amount of upper body tilt.

Your shoulders will rotate 90 degrees on the axis set by your posture. Both power and accuracy are the result of your arms swinging back on a slightly higher plane. Following the transition, as you swing down to the ball your arms will be able to swing more freely, thus enhancing the benefits of centrifugal force.

Good spine angles set at address allow the shoulders to rotate 90 degrees on the correct axis.

BOB'S LEVEL SHOULDER TURN

This is a good drill for preventing your left shoulder from dipping way under your right on the backswing. After setting your correct address posture and correct upper body tilt, think about working the shoulders back, as level as possible, to avoid the tendency of the left shoulder rotating under the right.

1 Set a good spine angle at address and place a club across your chest at a slight left-to-right diagonal. The clubhead should be on the left shoulder and the shaft touching the right upper arm. A proper shoulder rotation will bring the shaft to parallel at the top, making up the slight difference set by the diagonal placement.

2 Rotate your shoulders as level as possible, allowing the address tilt to dictate the axis.

3 As the shoulders complete their rotation, the club becomes almost parallel to the ground. If my left shoulder went under the right, the club incorrectly would have ended up pointing toward the ground.

PROBLEM 19
HIPS NOT LEVEL

Swaying off the ball and then rotating, or dipping your left knee on the backswing, results in the hips not staying level throughout your swing. Once a problem begins, it has to run its course.

The left hip is forced to rise at impact for the club to reach the ball. Shot problems vary from fat to thin, depending on when the hips briefly return to level in the downswing. This problem needs to be corrected because it adversely affects your balance and swing angles.

You suffer from this problem if your right hip is higher on the backswing and lower on the follow-through. The hips should be level throughout your swing.

TOUR CURE 19
KEEP YOUR BELT PARALLEL

Your hips must stay level as you swing back and then drive down through the ball. This way, your balance is maintained and your weight can shift properly, creating a power-producing impact position.

Unnecessary body movements, like raising the hips, waste power. Swaying back requires a forward sway on the way down, instead of maintaining a firm left side. Thinking about keeping your hips level also prevents the left knee from dipping. Try this drill to help level your hips.

Address the ball with proper posture. Place a club level across the front of your hips at your belt line.

Rotate back and through, keeping the club and your belt level and parallel to the ground. Feel your weight transfer from the left to the right on the backswing and back to a firm left side on the downswing. During a round, think about keeping your belt level throughout your swing.

PROBLEM 20
SHOULDER HITTING CHIN

Your shoulder bumping into your chin during the backswing restricts rotation and bumps the club off its correct swing plane. The greater the distance the shoulders can rotate, the farther your ball will travel.

This problem's origin began by misinterpreting the meaning of keeping your head down during the swing. Tucking the chin into the chest at address does not allow enough space for the shoulders to turn on the backswing.

Keeping your chin up at address helps solve the problem. However, as we discover below, the real cure comes from watching Jack Nicklaus.

TOUR CURE 20
NICKLAUS'S CHIN MOVEMENT

Instructor Jack Grout would hold the golden locks of a very young Jack Nicklaus during his swing, painfully emphasizing the virtues of maintaining a steady head. While his head should remain in relatively the same position during the swing, the chin does turn back to the right during the backswing.

His head turns to the right so much you would think Jack only sees the ball out of his left eye. In fact, the right eye also sees the ball over his nose.

Turning the chin makes room for the left shoulder to swing under it. This gives you an idea of how much of a level shoulder turn he makes. Think about turning your head from the time that you prepare to initiate your backswing. Turn the head back and then release it forward, following your shoulders on the downswing.

Turn your chin to make room for your left shoulder to swing under it.

PROBLEM 21
INCORRECT DOWNSWING TRANSITION

You would think from the quick, arm-dominated transitions I see that the ball has a mind of its own and wants to leave if you don't get back to it immediately. Trust me, your ball is not going anywhere until you make contact.

As you begin the transition to the downswing, your first movement dictates the rhythm and direction the club takes getting back to the ball. A quick downward motion led by the arms causes a slice. That's the result of a steep outside-to-inside swing path—often referred to as swinging over the top.

Target Line

TOUR CURE 21
LOWER BODY LEADS THE RETURN

Here is a good rule to remember: **The upper body leads the way on the backswing and the lower body leads the way on the downswing.** This choreographed movement creates the smooth, efficient swings you marvel at while watching the professionals.

The order of downward movement is:

- The hips begin their return to the ball while the shoulders continue rotating back, storing up maximum coiled energy.

- Continuing the hip rotation pulls the shoulders into the downswing, just as the shoulders pulled the hips into the backswing.

- This smoothly coordinated movement keeps you on plane and inside the target line, instead of crossing over the line as a shoulder-led transition would incorrectly do. The photos at right prove my point.

HIPS LEAD DOWNSWING TRANSITION

When Steve shot this action swing sequence, he said an entire roll of film was used just on my pause at the top. While this is a slight exaggeration, I do have a very quiet moment before beginning the downswing.

Look closely at my belt buckle for signs of how my transition begins. Notice it has moved toward the ball while my club position is still almost parallel. This hip-led transition smoothly puts me on the power track.

The clubface will be square at impact without having to make a jerky mid-course correction, which wastes precious clubhead speed.

PRACTICE TEE

I have several drills specifically designed to instill the correct feel for a transition that the lower body leads down to the ball. The most effective way to become accustomed to this feeling is to practice at home without a ball. The next time you go to the course, your swing should be smoother and more in sync.

KEEP THE LINE TIGHT DRILL

To feel how your transition should maximize the energy created by your backswing, buy a five-foot piece of inexpensive surgical-style rubber bungie cord. This is all you need for this drill.

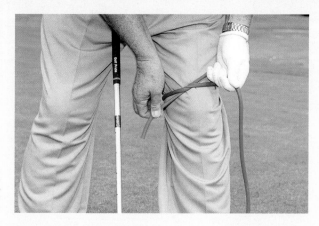

1 Tie the bungie cord to your left thigh. If you later need to adjust the amount of cord, do it by shortening the cord at your thigh.

2 Hold the cord's other end with your hands against the grip as you address the ball. Notice the cord is slack because we have not begun building backswing energy.

3 As you swing back, the slack is taken up and replaced by the tension felt as it stretches. Continue swinging back, simulating the top of your backswing or as far back as the cord will stretch.

4 I begin the transition by rotating my lower body toward the ball while still swinging my upper body back. Opposite-direction body movements maintain the tension in the cord—even increasing it. At the proper time, I let go and the tension releases the swing just like a catapult. The bungie cord, in reality, is the coiled body. Long-hitting players are adept at increasing this coiled energy even as the downswing begins.

This photo shows the problem caused by starting the transition with your upper body. The cord immediately goes slack, demonstrating the elimination of built-up energy and consequently the loss of club-head speed and distance. An added problem: The club will be outside of the swing plane and forced to cut across the ball at impact, causing a slice.

BROOM DRILL

A broom that has been cut down to the length of a golf club will help you learn how to make a transition led by your lower body. Here's what to do:

1 Assume your address position by standing with your derriere about 6 inches from a wall. Be sure to set the proper spine angle.

2 Swing the broom back as you would a golf club. At the point where your left arm becomes parallel to the ground, the broom should come in contact with the wall.

3 As you swing the broom shaft up to a vertical position, check to make sure the broom is still touching the wall.

4 A correct lower-body-led downswing will keep the broom staying on the wall to about hip high. Leaving the wall prior to hip high proves you began the transition incorrectly with your upper body.

DOWNSWING TO FOLLOW-THROUGH

Trust it! This is the best advice a professional can give once the downswing starts. If you reached the top of your backswing in good shape and then allowed your hips to lead the way down to the ball, you have completed the most potentially problem-filled portion of your swing. Now, just let it go.

With roughly one-half second to go from the top of the backswing to complete follow-through, you have very little choice if you plan on maintaining clubhead speed. Any mid-swing maneuver significantly slows the club, costing distance-producing energy.

Two of the most common problems members face during the downswing are understanding how to maintain linkage and when to release. Scott Hoch and Bob Murphy offer a variety of cures, followed by Martin Hall's intensive-care drills on the Practice Tee.

PROBLEM 22
LOSS OF LINKAGE

Attempting to correct downswing compensation problems prior to this point leads to throwing the club at the ball instead of keeping the upper body linked together. Break the triangular link between the club, hands, arms and shoulders, and I guarantee you will not be happy with the outcome.

Videotaping your swing and watching it in slow motion or frame by frame helps reveal if you lost this connection. Swinging in front of a mirror and stopping midway down also allows you to check your positions. Compare Casey's demonstrated position (left) with mine (right).

CLUB TRAILS BEHIND

SCOTT STAYS CONNECTED

The grip is behind the body, making it impossible to swing powerfully through impact. Throwing the club at the ball with the arms from this position will produce a very weak shot. The grip of the club should always be in front of your body to maintain the linkage.

Staying linked builds centrifugal force—the power developed during my downswing. Clubhead velocity increases rapidly as the shaft becomes parallel to the ground.

TOUR CURE 22
MAINTAIN THE TRIANGLE

The early morning dew flying off my club-head shows the powerful downward swing arc bringing the clubhead back to the ball. Look closely at the grip of the club. Notice its position in front of my body and within the triangle formed by my hands, arms and shoulder line.

This same triangular relationship began at address and continues throughout my entire swing. While the grip does not always point straight at my chest, it remains in front of my body. This is a powerful example of linkage.

BACKSWING LINKAGE

FOLLOW-THROUGH LINKAGE

PROBLEM 23
RELEASING EARLY

You can get away with an early release with a wood, but if you are a poor long iron player, this is probably the reason. While all good players maintain a wrist cock angle until the last possible moment in order to release powerfully through the ball, less-skilled players release their wrist cock prematurely.

Even with a wood, an early release will cost you distance, but the club's sweeping motion disguises the problem. Irons differ because they must be hit solidly. Flipping the hands through impact does not allow the left wrist to stay ahead of the clubhead. If you don't take divots with your irons, you are probably an early releaser.

An early release in action.

TOUR CURE 23
MAINTAIN WRIST COCK ANGLE

If you release early, begin thinking in terms of becoming a natural hitter. The wrist cock angle—formed by the back of your right forearm and hand—should be maintained until your swing releases it for you.

Skilled players tend to think of the golf swing as just that—a swing—while less-skilled players become determined to hit the ball. Skilled players allow centrifugal force to power their swings, and at impact the ball gets in the way.

Instead of trying to release their wrists, skilled players allow centrifugal force to pull them naturally into a release. This whips the clubhead through the ball, releasing the last bit of stored-up energy. A stop-action photo of a professional's swing will show a slight wrist cock angle (below) shortly after impact.

WRISTS COCKED

This is the wrist cock angle (dotted lines) to maintain.

DELAYED RELEASE

Notice Scott has not released his wrists just after impact. Release occurs later in the swing allowing centrifugal force to whip the clubhead through the ball creating power and accuracy.

PROBLEM 24
POWERLESS SWING

One reason golfers have problems developing power is that they concentrate on positions instead of creating movement in their swings. Golf is not a static sport. You don't connect the dots of various positions; you swing through them.

Another problem is the ball itself. It just sits there! In baseball, your response to a 100-mph fastball requires a split-second decision to take a rip at it, if you decide to swing. Golfers control the time element, and nothing happens until *you* begin the swing.

Sometimes a lackluster swing is the result, as demonstrated at right. There is no sense of anticipation of motion or athleticism about it. It just looks blah.

POWERLESS SWING

Here's a lackluster, powerless swing.

TOUR CURE 24
THINK BASEBALL

Most golfers have played some baseball as kids and have knowledge of what a rotational swing should feel like. Somehow that changes when you put a ball on a tee. I want you to recapture that feeling and put some power back into your swing.

Watch the pros on television preparing to drive on a par-5. If they plan on knocking it on in two shots, watch them look down the fairway with the club above waist high. They make a level baseball-type practice swing to instill this power producing feeling.

I use this same technique at clinics or whenever I try to help golfers put some power in their swings. Try this with me:

1 Begin by holding the club out in front of you, and have some flex in your knees. Your upper body stays tall. It should also be tall when you drop the club to the ground, even though you've bent at the waist.

2 Make your swing back (near right photo), and then swing the club back to the ball as if it were a baseball bat (far right photo). This is the key portion of the swing because all baseball players know how to hold the club back, even though their hips are moving toward the ball. Create this same feeling at transition.

3 In this baseball-type swing, you will find your wrists release by themselves as a result of centrifugal force (far left photo), just as Scott Hoch demonstrated in the last cure. Finally, the swing takes you all the way around to face the pitcher on your follow-through (near left photo). Now transfer this powerful baseball swing to the ground.

Swing
Cures:
Downswing
to Follow-
Through

PROBLEM 25
INCOMPLETE FOLLOW-THROUGH

Casey is demonstrating a follow-through position that did not finish the swing properly. That's the symptom. But if you finish like this, the reason is that your hips did not clear to the left, leaving no room for the arms to swing through.

If your transition began with your arms leading the way instead of your hips, this is the result, and it points out the importance of proper synchronization of the various moving body parts. Let's sweep out this position with the broom that I use in the cure.

TOUR CURE 25
SWING THE BROOM

In the first tournament I did for NBC-TV, I noticed that the players did one thing alike—they all had identical follow-throughs. Their address position and width of their stance varied and their swings were different, but every player drives through to his left leg and finishes facing the target standing straight.

A good player can do this because the hips clear out of the way prior to the arms swinging through. Centrifugal force then carries them the rest of the way. You can create this same feeling by swinging a broom from hip high on the backswing to hip high on the follow-through.

1 Start with a good address position and sweep the broom back to hip high.

2 Swing back down to the ball. Notice how the weight of the broom causes you to naturally rotate your hips to the left to reach the ball.

3 Swing the broom past impact to a hip-high follow-through position. The hips have cleared out of the way, just as they should in your swing.

4 Because your hips clear out of the way—as they did when swinging the broom—you will finish facing your target.

Before demonstrating some drills to help you with the part of the swing covered in this chapter, let's use the swing plane board to further understand how to generate power-producing centrifugal force.

SWING PLANE: DOWNSWING TO FINISH

1 Centrifugal force brings the club down the swing plane with an open face. Starting at this point, it will begin to square naturally as the swing continues without any help on your part.

2 The clubface continues to rotate toward square as it comes from inside the target line, thanks to your lower-body-led transition. If the upper body incorrectly began the transition, the club would be closed and outside the target line. If it opened at impact, you would slice. If it remained closed, you would pull the ball left.

3 Notice how centrifugal force squares the clubface at impact. The club head is travelling at maximum velocity, so this is not a position you can reach without:

- *Setting correct positions at address.*

- *Arriving at the correct position at the top.*

- *Beginning your downswing with your lower body.*

- *Trusting the swing the rest of the way.*

4 The club continues on plane past impact and the face begins to rotate to closed.

5 The finish position brings the club around the swing plane circle. When the energies of centrifugal force run out, the swing stops. Do not try to stop the swing; let that happen naturally. You should be facing your target at completion.

STEP AND SWING TRANSITION DRILL

Here is a bit of choreography to help you learn how the lower body transition should feel.

1 Begin with your setup position.

2 Move your feet together.

3 Move the club in front of your feet.

4 Swing the club back with your feet together.

5 Step the left foot forward to its original position before you bring your hands down.

6 Swing the club down. The key here is to step and then swing for the proper lower-body-led transition. If you swing and step, you made an incorrect upper body transition.

TOUR
Cures

PREVENT CASTING DRILL

To stop casting the club, you have to develop the feeling of the triangular relationship between the hands and shoulders. For the first part of the swing, the clubhead and left shoulder must remain the same distance apart. The clubhead is moved down with the body. You do not move it down with the hands and arms.

Golfers whose distance between the clubhead and left shoulder widens before this swing position have a casting problem, which this drill will cure.

1 I take a rubber iron cover, which you can find at golf specialty stores, and attach it to a dog leash.

Long-ball hitters maintain this distance as long as possible. Why? Because, theoretically, if someone cut the cord with a pair of scissors, the clubhead would come flying through the ball at maximum velocity.

2 I put the iron cover on the club and take the club to the top of my backswing. I wrapped the dog leash under my left shoulder and back to the grip end of the club. This sets the triangle and the all-important distance between the clubhead and the left shoulder.

3 As the hips move toward the target, the hands will move down about 12 inches, but the line keeps the distance between the clubhead and left shoulder constant. Notice the grip of the club stays in front of my body. As you swing for real, the distance must not get wider.

POWER BUILDING MOTION DRILL

As Bob Murphy stated earlier in this chapter, the reason some members have trouble developing power in their swings is that they just shuffle through it. Bob's baseball swing is a good drill to put some "oomph" in it. Swinging a rope at home is also helpful.

Remember: The body leads the downswing, not the arms. If you have trouble making a complete follow-through, your body didn't lead your arms through the swing. You can't apply arm leverage to the rope; the body must wind and unwind to move it.

Think of your body as winding and unwinding. Your body should lead the downswing, not your arms.

3 BALL FLIGHT, TERRAIN AND ROUGH CURES

"It is nothing new or original to say that golf is played one stroke at a time. But it took me many years to realize it." —Bobby Jones

Golf **is** played one stroke at a time, and because the golfer with the lowest score wins, accumulating extra strokes along the way is not in your best interest. Therefore, *TOUR Cures* will now turn to help correct your individual shot problems.

This chapter covers specific ball flight problems requiring professional expertise, terrain changes and cures to help free your ball from the rough. Our four professionals, who also are your fellow PGA TOUR Partners Club members, provide the needed cures to bring this part of your game back to health.

"When you are having trouble and topping the ball, it means the ground is moving on you." —Chi Chi Rodriguez

IN THIS SECTION

BALL FLIGHT PROBLEMS

- Slicing

- Hooking

- Shanking

- Toe Hits

- Skied Shots

- Worm Burners

- Fat Shots & Other Misses

- Poor Distance

- Practice Tee

UNEVEN TERRAIN PROBLEMS

- Falling Back on Uphill Shots

- Can't Get the Ball Airborne from Downhill Lies

- Chunking Above Your Feet Lies

- Thin Right Shots When the Ball is Below Your Feet

- Practice Tee

ROUGH CURES

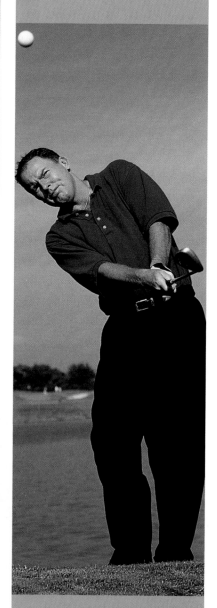

- Rough Misunderstanding

- Off-Line Shots

- Can't Get Out of the Rough

- Can't Stop the Ball on the Green

- Practice Tee

BALL FLIGHT PROBLEMS

The PGA TOUR media guide states that "Scott Hoch may be the PGA TOUR's most consistent player since joining the TOUR in 1980." Can you think of anyone better to correct your ball flight problems?

Playing in weekly pro-ams, Scott has seen just about any shot imaginable and some that are better off not even being talked about. To help his amateur partners get through the round, he regularly offers quick tips and provides professional advice on what they should ultimately work on to correct their problems.

With Martin Hall's Practice Tee suggestions, you will have ample information here to solve those nagging ball flight problems such as slicing, hooking, skying, fat and low shots, toe hits, and the one problem that destroys all confidence in your game—shanking. We begin with slicing.

PROBLEM 26
SLICING

More golfers slice than hook, so if you're a slicer you have plenty of company. Slicing can always be traced to one of two problems: mistakes at address, or swing mechanics problems that bring the clubhead from outside-in and cause it to slice across the ball.

The side of the tee box you choose also plays a role. Notice below how Casey is demonstrating from the far left of the tee—the spot most slicers choose to compensate for their left-to-right ball flight. Depending on the severity of your slice, this does not provide enough leeway for a slicing ball to land in the fairway.

If you teed up on the left side while aiming your club toward the center, this can also be part of the problem. Your lower body is probably aimed down the left side while the club is aimed to the center. This "open" position may be responsible for a bigger slice than normal.

TOUR CURE 26
QUICK AND LONG TERM CURES

If you want to hit your second shot from the fairway, here are two quick cures for your slicing problem: First, tee the ball on the right side of the tee box and aim left; second, slightly close the club at address.

QUICK CURE: TEE ON THE RIGHT AND AIM LEFT

You double the amount of fairway to work with by teeing right and aiming left, provided you have made no other changes. The ball can fly toward the fairway's left side before slicing back across. Only you know how much you slice, so decide where your aiming starting point should be to compensate for the flight path.

QUICK CURE: TURN TOE CLOSED

Turning the toe of the club slightly closed (so it looks like it's pointing left) before you grip the club will also help. However, if you grip before closing, the club-face returns to meet the ball in the old impact position.

LONG TERM CURE: UNLOCK YOUR LEFT SIDE

If you have corrected your address flaws and basic swing mechanics and you're still battling a slice, you may be locking up your left side. Most slicers incorrectly lock their left knee at impact, promoting a big cut.

During pro-ams I work with slicers on maintaining a flexed left side at address through follow-through. Notice the amount of knee flex (above) as the club speeds toward the ball. The therapy: Make sure both knees retain their address flex as you transition to the downswing.

Ball Flight, Terrain and Rough Cures: Ball Flight Problems

PROBLEM 27
HOOKING

If you hook the ball, you are doing some things a lot better than if you sliced. For one thing, unless you have a severe duck hook, you will get more distance even though you seldom find the short grass.

Some of the reasons contributing to unacceptable right-to-left ball flight (a hook) are mistakes made both at address and in swing mechanics.

You may also be contributing to the hooks by teeing from the right side of the tee, believing the ball has room to hook across the fairway. Usually what happens is that you position your body to the right side of the fairway but aim the club toward the center. This closes your stance and encourages a hook more severe than the one you might really have.

TOUR CURE 27
QUICK AND LONG TERM CURES

We don't see as many hookers as slicers. Because you are doing a lot more right than wrong, your problems should be easier to cure. I have a quick cure along with a long-term cure.

Only you know how severe your hook is. Teeing from the left side of the tee provides double the fairway to work with. Your ball can start out right across the fairway and then has twice the room to hook back.

Adjust your aiming starting point to compensate for your hook. If your ball flight is just a slight draw, try teeing up from the left center of the tee box.

QUICK CURE: TEE LEFT AND AIM RIGHT

LONG TERM CURE: POINT V'S TOWARD THE CENTER

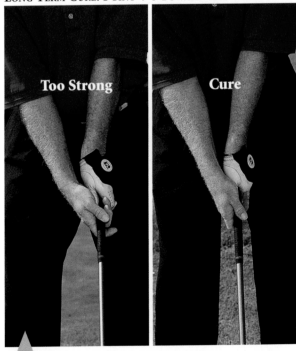

Too Strong

Cure

V's in your grip that point outside the right shoulder can be the problem. I suggest that if you hook, it is perfectly acceptable to adjust the V's so they point more toward the center of your body.

LONG TERM CURE: DELAY FOREARM ROTATION

Drawing the ball requires the right forearm rotating over the left through impact. Accomplished players who are drawing the ball more than they want may be releasing the clubhead through the ball too early.

Changing the route of the club back to the ball is not a good idea. Delaying the rotation with your grip (see photo) provides a better cure. Gripping harder with the last three fingers of the left hand makes it difficult for the right forearm to turn over the left.

Ball Flight, Terrain and Rough Cures: Ball Flight Problems

PROBLEM 28
THE DREADED SHANKS

It's not the hard-right ball flight or the disgusting sound that identifies you as a shanker, it's the reaction of your former playing partners. The rest of the golf world is afraid shanking may be contagious, so your friends stay away and no one wants to hear or know anything about it.

Actually, a shank is very close to being a solid shot, but developing a shank can turn you into a psychological mess. It's caused when the clubhead is not released at impact. Shanking takes two forms: Either the shot goes immediately to the right, indicating the ball met the hosel, or the shot goes hard left, indicating the ball was trapped between the hosel and clubface.

TOUR CURE 28
HALF-INCH FROM A GOOD SHOT

When I said shanking was close to being a good shot, here's why: Golfers who draw the ball have an open clubface that closes at impact. When you shank, it's likely you are standing too close to the ball; and the hosel, which is slightly ahead prior to impact, hits the ball before the clubface does.

My cure is to try a simple approach. Stand a half-inch farther from the ball. This puts the ball right in the center of the clubface at impact. The cure for your occasional shanks may be that simple. Martin Hall has a weight shift suggestion in the Practice Tee at the end of this chapter.

Typical shank impact.

Step back a half-inch to put the ball in the center of the clubface at impact.

PROBLEM 29

TOE HITS

A toe hit is just the opposite of a shank. Reaching for the ball is the usual reason, but spinning through the shot may also be causing it. The club approaches the ball from outside the target line and abruptly goes inside, making contact with only the toe.

You lose your grip and think that was the problem, but it isn't. The real reason is the ball impacting just the far edge of the club's toe. Weak shots to the right or left are a result of the clubface twisting open after toe-only impact.

TOUR CURE 29

PLACE BALL ON HEEL

If you are spinning around the shot and not following the swing plane and basic fundamentals we covered in Chapter 2, my suggestion is to begin there. But if you feel that spinning is not the problem for occasional toe hits, the cure is relatively simple.

Address the ball as you normally would, then move closer by about a half-inch, at which point the ball will be on the heel of the clubface. This will not cause a toe hitter to shank because your problem is that you don't stand close enough to the ball to begin with.

Move a half-inch closer to the ball to avoid toe hits.

Ball Flight,
Terrain
and
Rough
Cures:
Ball Flight
Problems

81

PROBLEM 30
SKIED SHOTS

How disappointing! You thought you made the perfect swing and when you looked up the ball was gaining altitude faster than a shuttle launch. The problem is either simple or more complicated.

- Simple: The ball is teed too high.

- Complicated: You are hitting down on the ball.

TOUR CURE 30
LOWER THE TEE AND SWEEP THROUGH THE SHOT

Tee your ball lower, to meet the club's sweetspot.

Skying is easy to cure if you are teeing the ball too high. The old adage "tee it high and let it fly" only works if you play the ball farther ahead in your stance, allowing impact on the upswing. Additional distance can be gained due to the increased amount of topspin.

However, if you sky the ball, tee it lower so it can be met by the club's sweetspot. Lining up the top of the driver with the ball's equator is a good measuring idea.

If you are hitting down on the ball, you probably have the same problem as hitting the ball fat with an iron. TOUR Cure 32 helps with that problem.

PROBLEM 31
LOW TRAJECTORY

Casey is really a good golfer but he's demonstrating the unfortunate outcome of a low ball trajectory off this elevated tee. The ball went into the water because impact was on its top portion or upper hemisphere. More topspin was created so it flew too low and, in this case, it took a watery plunge.

Another problem can also be attributed to looking up too soon. In either case, hitting the ball low after making a good swing is a problem that can be easily cured.

TOUR CURE 31
PROPER BALL POSITION

Here's another "take two aspirins and call me in the morning" cure: Before trying anything drastic, I would go for the most likely cure—adjusting your ball position.

My shot (above) is climbing because impact was at the bottom of my swing arc. Chapter 2 covers this in detail. For driving, the correct ball position is opposite your left armpit. As the driver sweeps through the ball, clubface loft will launch it on the correct trajectory.

If you are looking up too soon, you will hit the ball off your right side instead of swinging through it and naturally coming up on your follow-through. Your shoulders turning through the ball will pull your head up at the proper time without any help.

Ball Flight,
Terrain
and
Rough
Cures:
Ball Flight
Problems

PROBLEM 32
FAT SHOTS, TOPPED SHOTS AND LEFT AND RIGHT MISSES

Hitting the ball fat in the fairway can be related to the problem of skying it off the tee. The photo shows a divot behind a teed ball. In the fairway your iron-caused divot would be larger and deeper. If you hit it fat or top it, you are likely moving your head up and down. A swaying head causes missing left or right.

To diagnose these problems, have someone watch only your head as you swing. Not only will they be able to detect head movement but they can also apply my cure.

TOUR CURE 32
MAINTAIN A STEADY HEAD

Your head is the center of your swing. It must remain steady so you can swing back from the ball and then return to it with everything in the correct position. A head moving up or down or swaying left or right does not provide the constant center for the turn axis. As a result, swing compensations have to be made to return to the ball.

The cure is to have someone put a finger on your head as you swing. This provides instant feedback because you feel the finger move if the head moves. Work on maintaining a steady head/finger relationship. Virtually all fat, skied and sculled shots are caused by this problem.

PROBLEM 33
POOR DISTANCE AND LOSS OF FEEL

All golfers lose distance and feel at some point. Of course it affects players of different skill levels in proportionate ways. It's frustrating because you really do not have a clue as to what the problem is.

The problem always has something to do with one of the basic fundamentals. So shrug your shoulders, shake your head, take a deep, relaxing breath, and I'll show you my own personal cure when this happens to me.

TOUR CURE 33
RETURN TO THE BASICS

When I start to lose my feel, I don't rip my game apart during a round. That's one mistake amateurs make. We all hit bad shots, but professionals only make major changes on the range after the round.

This is how I try to feel my way back to my normal swing:

1 The first three feet in the backswing is important. I concentrate on a slower pace back so I don't rush the backswing. As I take the club back, my shoulders lead the way and the hips resist. I'm more of a left-sided golfer, so I keep more weight on my left foot because I like to hit lower, punch-type shots. I feel a firm left side at the top of my backswing with both knees flexed.

2 My left hip starts the downswing as it rotates toward the target.

3 I want to finish facing the target.

Is there anything more frustrating than watching your ball fly on the wrong trajectory as if it has a mind of its own? Along with Scott's outstanding cures, I'll provide some additional help on a few of the ball flight problems to get you back on track.

SLICING

If you're slicing, you primarily deal with an open clubface at impact. This can be part of the cause/effect syndrome. Mistakes made at address, take-away and transition come back to haunt you during ball flight.

If you are sure the slicing problem is not related to a problem in setup or the early part of the swing, here are some additional cures to help square the clubface at impact.

STRENGTHEN YOUR GRIP

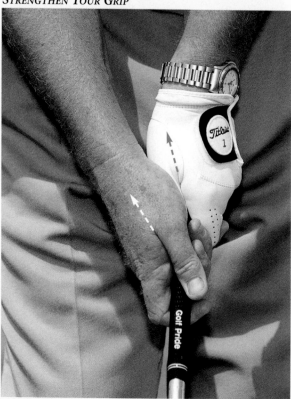

Strengthening does not mean grip tighter. It refers only to the position of your hands on the grip. The V's tell the tale. If they are pointing to your chin or left side of your body, you found the problem.

Simply shift your hands toward the right so the V's point more toward your right shoulder. This is a stronger position that encourages more of a draw.

TWO CURES IN ONE

1

2

These photos illustrate two cures for slicing—(1) widening the release and (2) rolling the arms through the ball. Notice how extended my arms are, both on the downswing and on the follow-through positions.

This creates a greater distance for the clubhead to square to the ball. At the same time, you can see how my right forearm has rotated over the left through impact. Try some hip-high to hip-high practice swings to develop this double feeling.

HOOKING

Cures for hooking tend to be opposite of those for slicing. Hooks are caused by a closed clubface at impact. Once again you should review the cures in Chapter 2 for problems both at address and in various parts of the swing.

However, if those are not the problems, try these new and improved cures.

WEAKEN GRIP

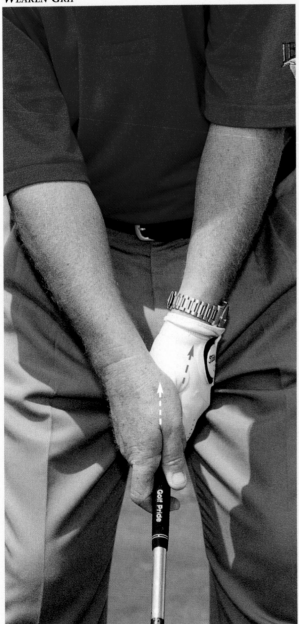

Scott showed you how to weaken your grip in Cure 27. Here it is again to save you the time of turning back to see it. If the V's are pointed toward the right side of your body or past it, shift the hands so the V's now point more toward the center of your body.

SHORTEN THE RELEASE AREA

Notice how I have shortened the downswing portion of the swing (above) compared to the anti-slice swing. The reason is that I want to delay the ability of the right arm to roll over the left too early in the release.

Keeping the right knuckles under for as long as possible (top) further ensures the right forearm has not rotated over the left through impact. This delay stops the clubface from closing early and should straighten your hook to a slight draw or even a slight fade. Practice a few half swings to develop this feeling.

Ball Flight, Terrain and Rough Cures: Ball Flight Problems

SHANKING

Here is a cure to go along with what Scott said about changing your position relative to the ball: Put your weight on your heels.

As you compare the two photos, notice how by lifting my toes the weight goes slightly back on my heels. Scott told you that a shank is almost a good shot requiring just a slight distance adjustment. Placing weight on your heels can move the club's position just enough to allow ball contact with the face instead of the hosel.

UNEVEN TERRAIN PROBLEMS

Golf is played on terrain shaped both by nature and by the course architect. From an uneven lie, you must adapt to the slope of the ground or face the consequences.

Some members may have problems adjusting to the situations found in this chapter because of their inability to find a way to practice the uneven shot. Martin Hall suggests a cure for this problem in the Practice Tee.

But first, fan favorite Chi Chi Rodriguez escorts you around the course in search of some uneven lies. Members who can only play once a week or less may be overlooking adjustments in technique that are second nature to professionals.

PROBLEM 34
FALLING BACK ON UPHILL SHOTS

Do you fall back after hitting from an uphill lie, or does your ball fly high but not long? Golfers typically encounter three problems when hitting up a slope: (1) improper club selection; (2) not adjusting for the slope; (3) not staying in balance throughout the swing.

Patrick, an assistant pro at Arnold Palmer's Bay Hill Club and a Partners Club member, demonstrates the problem—a setup with shoulders that are not parallel to the slope and hands that are back behind the ball. Casey demonstrates that improperly setting up for the slope results in a loss of balance after impact. A high, weak shot, or even one hit into the hill, is the result, depending on where the ball was positioned.

While pre-setting your weight on the right foot is desirable, failing to set and then maintain your shoulders parallel to the slope creates a big problem: Falling away after impact.

Club selection is equally important. Selecting the same club that you would use for a flat lie is the wrong choice. Uphill slopes naturally create more loft because of the launch angle, so a less-lofted club is a better choice, such as a 5-iron instead of a 6-iron, or a 7- or 8-iron instead of a 9-iron.

A bad setup: shoulders not parallel to the slope and hands behind the ball.

If you don't set up right on a slope, you will surely lose your balance after impact and make a poor shot.

TOUR CURE 34
MAKE THE HILL DO THE WORK

I'm using a wood combined with a half-swing as a teaching practice aid to help cure your uphill problems. The key to shots from sloping terrain is to make the slope do your work. In this case, the hill and your body position combine to easily create loft, so your task is to tailor it to your need.

The half-shot allows me to concentrate on regaining control of my balance, and the wood takes care of the lower trajectory. The distance should dictate the club selection, but practicing with the wood will quickly develop your skills. I'm only making a half-swing, but as you become more skilled at maintaining your balance, the swing can be increased to at least three-quarters.

ADDRESS

- Choke down.

- Ball back in stance.

- Shoulders are parallel to the up-slope.

- Weight on the right foot.

BALANCED BACKSWING

- Shoulders stay parallel to the slope.

- The half-swing allows you to stay in control.

- Be sure the toe of the wood is pointing up.

BALANCED IMPACT

- Weight remains mostly on the inside of right foot.

- Notice the shoulders return to the same parallel to the up-slope position.

- The lower-trajectory wood started the ball off lower.

- My balance is under control.

BALANCED HALF FOLLOW-THROUGH

- I finish my half-swing facing the target.

- Club finishes waist high.

- The half-swing allowed me to transfer the appropriate amount of weight to the left side while maintaining my balance.

Ball Flight, Terrain and Rough Cures: Uneven Terrain Problems

PROBLEM 35
CAN'T GET BALL AIRBORNE FROM DOWNHILL LIE

A golf ball is like a clock. Always hit it at 6 o'clock and make it go toward 12 o'clock. But make sure you're in the same time zone.

Getting the ball airborne from a downhill lie is one of golf's most technically demanding shots. Staying in balance is important because the slope fights a normal weight transfer.

Casey is trying to brace himself against gravity by keeping his weight on the back leg when just the opposite is needed. As a result, he remains vertically upright during impact and follow-through, making it impossible to hit down on the ball. This is impossible when you have to fight for balance, but my cure will help get your ball airborne from both slight and steep inclines. Below is my cure for a relatively slight slope, and because the hills are not very steep here in Florida, I'll comment on severe downhill lies as well. Both cases require a downward attack angle, instead of trying to sweep the ball down the slope.

The back leg is not the place for your weight (left). You won't be able to hit down on the ball, and balancing will be tough (right).

TOUR CURE 35
BRACE YOURSELF TO HIT DOWN

FOR SLIGHT SLOPES

- Choose a more lofted club than the distance indicates because the slope closes a 4-iron to a 3-iron's loft at impact.

- Play the ball back in your stance and place your weight on the downhill foot and keep it there during your entire swing as a brace.

- Hit down on the ball, allowing the club's loft to do the work.

- Trying to lift the ball leads to the club passing over it, resulting in a miss or a thin shot.

Severe Downhill Lies

Here's how fellow TOUR pro Dana Quigley handled a 180-yard, steep downhill shot.

1 - Half Backswing

- Dana widened his stance to help stay parallel to the slope.

- His half backswing helps him remain balanced with his downhill leg as the brace.

- He choked down on the grip because the ground arrives sooner on a steep slope downswing.

- This is one of the few situations where you swing with only hands and arms (notice the wrist cock).

2 - Aggressive Downswing

- Weight stays on downhill leg.

- Dana stays in control but aggressively makes a downward swing.

3 - Airborne

- The ball is climbing off this severe downhill slope.

- Dana stayed down and impacted the ball below its equator, enabling it to gain both height and distance.

4 - Balanced Follow-Through

- Weight is firmly on downhill leg.

- Dana is in balance, and finishes high and around.

PROBLEM 36
CHUNKING THE BALL ABOVE YOUR FEET

Even though the ball is only slightly higher than his feet, Casey demonstrates why some members hit the ground prior to impacting the ball. Notice he's gripping the club at the end of the shaft. He should be gripping the club lower on the grip to compensate for the ball being above a normally flat lie.

Because Casey hasn't adjusted the length of the club to compensate for the higher lie, the clubhead hits the ground prior to the ball. This force opens the clubface and bends Casey's left arm, sending the ball short and off line. When you do not play as frequently as a pro, it's easy to forget these slight, yet vital, adjustments.

Look at Casey's lower body. It's too active through the shot. His swaying legs make it difficult to crisply make contact with the ball.

Note the problems on this swing: Gripping the club at the end of the shaft (left), which makes the clubhead hit the ground too early (right). The lower body here is too active.

TOUR CURE 36
LOWER BODY STAYS QUIET

When your feet are lower than the ball, a draw (right-to-left ball flight) is the usual result. Unless you aim right of the target to compensate, the ball will finish left. Once your aim is correct, the next step is to choke down and maintain a quiet lower body through the shot.

Compare my post-impact position (main photo here) to Casey's position. My clubface was able to close normally; Casey's clubface opened when it collided with the ground. I took a divot, but only after the club met the ball. Notice my hands are choked down to the bottom of the grip—effectively shortening the club.

BACKSWING

For this wedge, I only needed a 9 o'clock length backswing. Notice my quiet knees remained parallel to my target line. My shoulders and arms hit this shot.

FOLLOW-THROUGH

A high finish after hitting down on the ball provides the trajectory this wedge shot required. My hips pulled my quiet legs into the follow-through.

PROBLEM 37
THIN RIGHT SHOTS BELOW YOUR FEET

Casey is demonstrating a problem he had when his handicap was higher. If you hit a thin shot to the right when the ball is below your feet, the problem begins with your spine angle.

Casey's erect-posture swing (near-right photo) results in the ball heading off line to the right (far-right photo), indicating an open clubface at impact. The flatter swing plane caused by his upright position is responsible.

A more vertical swing is the desired result, causing a fade. If you are an ex-slicer, you have worked hard to avoid just that, but in this case a fade indicates a well-struck shot.

TOUR CURE 37
BEND MORE AND AIM LEFT

When the ball is below your feet, an alarm should go off in your head as a reminder to correctly set your address angle. All good golf shots require setting the correct angle to accommodate the lie. Maintaining this angle during the shot provides a constant axis for the shoulders to turn on.

Part of the problem may be that, while professionals play almost every day, you may play only once a week or less. The finer points of the game are difficult to remember, especially when you become distracted when facing similar lies to those found in this chapter. Casey's upright address position demonstrated that.

CORRECT ADDRESS ANGLE

Even with the ball below my feet I can still set the proper spine angle and knee flex at address. I bend more for steeper slopes. The thin shot is eliminated because I make good contact with the ball.

BALL POSITION

Gauge the bottom of the swing arc for the club you choose. Aim to the left of your target to compensate for the slope.

PRACTICE TEE

Finding a way to practice your uneven lie shots is not that easy. It's not as if you can just leisurely walk onto the course with a shag bag and practice hitting uphill shots or those with the ball lower than your feet.

I have a practice suggestion: If you check with your local golf range

management, they might see the wisdom in accommodating this very needed practice situation. In fact, you can show them this Practice Tee segment, because we are about to show you our solution. Let's begin with uphill shots.

UPHILL SHOTS DRILL

Many ranges have hitting station platforms. To demonstrate our shots, we propped up one end of the platform. For the uphill shots, the front is propped up so I can practice swinging uphill.

SPINE DRILL

The simple way for you to align yourself properly to the hill is to stand so that your spine becomes perpendicular to the hill at address. For a teaching aid, I went to a home improvement store and assembled a T-stick made with PVC pipe.

SPINE PERPENDICULAR

The lower end of the T-stick rests on the raised platform. When the vertical portion of the T-stick bisects the middle of my body, my spine is aligned perpendicular to the slope.

INCORRECT SPINE POSITION

The pipe may be bisecting my forehead, but my lower body is incorrectly ahead of the stick. This indicates my spine angle is not perpendicular but points at an angle that will create too much loft.

CLUB PATH DRILL

With your spine set perpendicular to the hill, swing up the slope (above), which automatically adds loft to the shot. Choose a less lofted club to compensate (6-iron instead of 7-iron).

Do not fight the slope. Make it work for you by swinging *up* the slope, not into it. Keep the weight on your back foot, with your spine perpendicular. As a result, the club can follow the uphill slope, square to the ball, and then curve along the swing arc toward the inside after impact (photos at left).

Swing slowly at first, staying in control, while developing a feel for your balance. Increase the speed of the swing with a faster body rotation, not just with your arms.

DOWNHILL LIES

Position the ball off the left side of your face.

There is very little weight shift, if any, off the left-braced leg on the backswing. Consequently, you will not be able to stay in control if you make more than a 9 o'clock backswing. From that position, follow the slope with the swing as I'm doing here.

The cure for hitting the ball in the air off downhill lies begins once again with establishing a perpendicular spine. This puts considerable weight on your left foot and, as Chi Chi pointed out, the left leg acts as a brace for the swing.

DOWNHILL BRACE DRILL

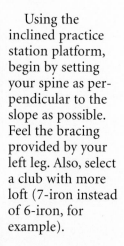

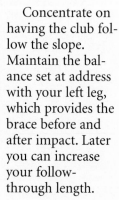

Using the inclined practice station platform, begin by setting your spine as perpendicular to the slope as possible. Feel the bracing provided by your left leg. Also, select a club with more loft (7-iron instead of 6-iron, for example).

Concentrate on having the club follow the slope. Maintain the balance set at address with your left leg, which provides the brace before and after impact. Later you can increase your follow-through length.

BALL ABOVE YOUR FEET

Some instructors suggest you hit balls above your feet to eliminate slicing tendencies, because the more rounded swing encourages a draw. That is yet another reason to convince your range manager to set some practice platforms on a tilt!

When the ball is above your feet, you need to make three immediate changes to your normal setup:

1 Choke down on the grip to shorten the club length.

2 Stand more erect with your spine. The weight should be a little more toward your heels to encourage this posture.

3 Standing more erect causes the ball to travel right to left, so adjust your aim more to the right to compensate. The more lofted the club, the more you will draw it.

CHOKE DOWN

Choke down, stand more erect and put your weight on your heels when hitting a ball above your feet.

ROUNDED SWING DRILL

This drill provides the feeling of the rounded swing.

- Swing the club back to about a three-quarter back-swing.

- Swing down and through, matching the back-swing length with your follow-through.

- Stay in balance and concentrate on feeling the weight toward the back of your feet.

If you maintained the spine angle set at address and shortened the club by choking down, you can scratch the symptom of chunking the shot off your problem list.

Ball Flight, Terrain and Rough Cures: Uneven Terrain Problems

BALL BELOW YOUR FEET

Shots hit with the ball below your feet will fade slightly because of a more upright swing. However, the amount of draw from a ball struck above your feet is greater than the amount of fade when struck below your feet. Take this into consideration when adjusting your aim for a shot to the left of your target.

Make these adjustments from your basic setup position:

1 Grip the club all the way to the end of the butt to effectively lengthen the shaft (inset photo).

2 Bend over the ball from your hips, setting a greater spine angle (photo above). You will feel the weight more on your toes to maintain balance.

3 With increased bending, a slightly steeper swing plane develops and the ball fades.

VERTICAL SWING DRILL

This drill provides the feeling of a more vertical swing.

1Swing the club back to about a three-quarter backswing. Swing down and through, matching the backswing length with your follow-through. Stay in balance and concentrate on feeling the weight toward the toes.

2If you maintained your spine angle set at address and lengthened the club by gripping it to the end, you can scratch the symptom of thinning the shot off your problem list.

ROUGH CURES

Scott Hoch's early PGA TOUR career made him the likely choice to be our rough expert. When he first joined the TOUR his driving accuracy was, in his word, "terrible!" Landing in the rough was a frequent occurrence; yet he still ranked among the leaders in reaching the greens in regulation (GIR).

Scott adapted to the situation and turned his driving weakness into a plus. Over the years, his driving accuracy has improved, but when he ends up in the rough these days he has the confidence to hit a lot of greens.

Scott takes you inside the ropes to cure your rough problems. And Martin Hall has an outstanding tip on the Practice Tee to help you adapt to the longer grass.

PROBLEM 38
MISUNDERSTANDING THE ROUGH

Part of your problem in the rough could be that you don't have a clear understanding of what's needed to get on the green or back in the fairway. All too many times I watch my pro-am partners trying to hit a shot out of the rough as if they had a perfect fairway lie. Unfortunately, that's an invitation to try it again.

Our friend Casey is positive that the 3-iron he would normally use from this distance is the correct club to hit from the rough. Casey has become a good golfer and really knows that a more lofted iron or even a wood is a better choice. Instead of his thumb pointing up, it should be pointing down for selecting the 3-iron.

Here are some other problems that are associated with not understanding how to correctly play from the rough:

* The same club will produce different results from the rough and fairway. Grass gets between the clubface and ball, restricting backspin.

* Not playing for a lot of run when the ball lands. The ball reacts this way because it flies on a lower trajectory with less spin. After landing, it releases and rolls instead of checking and stopping.

* Not adapting your swing to the rough. This invites the clubface to open as the grass wraps around the hosel, sending the ball off-line.

TOUR CURE 38
ROUGH BASIC TRAINING

Adapting your game to hit from the rough begins with assessing your lie. If the rough is not deep and you can easily get your club on the ball, you don't need to make many changes. If the grass is higher and partially covers the ball, try these cures to play the shot.

CLOSE THE FACE AND MAKE A STEEPER SWING

POWER THROUGH TO FINISH

When the grass is thicker, I play for a lot of run. I slightly shut the clubface and then make a steeper swing than normal down to impact. This creates less drag on the club from the taller grass.

If you take a normal swing through a thick lie, a lot of grass becomes trapped between the clubface and ball. This can turn the clubface open and the ball will come out either sideways or baffled, lacking power and energy.

Never quit on a shot hit from the rough. Accelerate through impact and make a complete follow-through.

PROBLEM 39
OFF-LINE SHOTS FROM THE ROUGH

Casey is demonstrating the problem of the clubface opening at impact as he hits from the rough. Notice his feet are aligned for a shot down the center of Bay Hill's sixth hole (dotted line). However, the ball is not headed in that direction (red line).

Grass wrapped around his 3-iron, opening the face and sending the ball weakly to the right. The problem began with club selection. Hitting long irons out of the rough is not a good play.

A 5- or 7-wood would have been a better choice from this distance. The wood goes through the grass a little easier. If Casey were closer to the green, he could select an 8-iron (instead of a 7-iron) and close the clubface down.

TOUR CURE 39
BALL BACK IN STANCE AND HOLD ON

The cure for off-line shots begins with club selection and continues to address.

- Shut the club down and aim left of your target.

- Try not to tighten your grip, but make sure it's firm.

- Play the ball back in your stance to encourage a steeper, descending swing path. Less grass gets between the clubface and ball.

- Playing the ball back in the stance will make it go slightly right. Adapt by aiming more to the left.

- Accelerate to allow the clubhead to power its way along the natural swing arc.

- For skilled players, use this technique for a lie that is not too good, but not too severe.

- Less skilled players should apply this technique even when the rough is not deep.

Play the ball back in your stance.

Ball Flight,
Terrain
and
Rough
Cures:
Rough
Cures

PROBLEM 40
CAN'T GET OUT OF THE ROUGH

Poor golf course management has a lot to do with problems some players have in the rough. Failing to understand that a reasonable objective might be to get back in the fairway, it's not uncommon to see some golfers try to pull off a career shot from very tall grass.

You don't want to hit the ball only 10 yards, but that's what happens by trying to hit a 4-iron or 5-iron out of a bad lie. Just like Casey's ball, it might not even get out of the rough.

Course management and technique are equally important. Have you considered the following when playing a shot out of the rough?

Q If your home course has bentgrass and you are playing a course with a bermuda grass rough, do you understand the difference?

A Bermuda is thicker and harder to hit out of because the ball drops to the bottom.

Q Do you know how hard to hit the ball?

A This takes practice and experience. The key is to accelerate through the shot. The descending swing path I illustrated in Cure 34 is not the same as hitting down on the ball. Hitting down often results in not being able to follow-through. Decelerating is fatal to successfully hitting from the rough.

TOUR CURE 40
PICK A REALISTIC TARGET

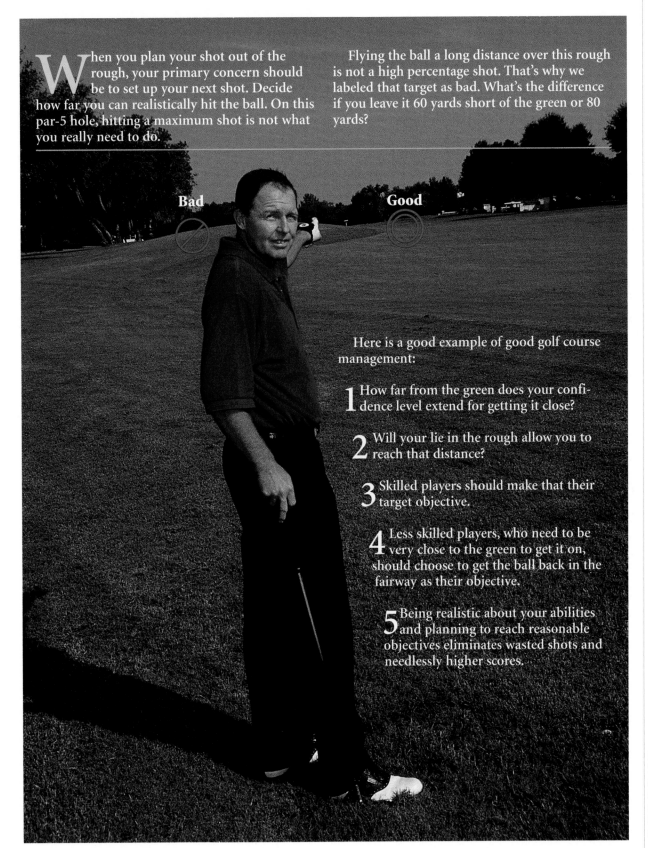

When you plan your shot out of the rough, your primary concern should be to set up your next shot. Decide how far you can realistically hit the ball. On this par-5 hole, hitting a maximum shot is not what you really need to do.

Flying the ball a long distance over this rough is not a high percentage shot. That's why we labeled that target as bad. What's the difference if you leave it 60 yards short of the green or 80 yards?

Bad

Good

Here is a good example of good golf course management:

1 How far from the green does your confidence level extend for getting it close?

2 Will your lie in the rough allow you to reach that distance?

3 Skilled players should make that their target objective.

4 Less skilled players, who need to be very close to the green to get it on, should choose to get the ball back in the fairway as their objective.

5 Being realistic about your abilities and planning to reach reasonable objectives eliminates wasted shots and needlessly higher scores.

PROBLEM 41
BALL GOES TOO FAR AND DOESN'T STOP

Casey hit a flier out of the rough. Instead of the ball checking up and stopping close to the pin, it released after landing and rolled off the green. The problem is not figuring the additional roll into the shot.

Hitting the ball from the fairway allows the clubface to cleanly impact the ball. For higher lofted clubs, the ball runs up the clubface and gathers backspin. When the ball lands, the applied backspin bites into the green and stops the ball where it lands (or within a few feet).

When grass gets between the clubface and ball, as it does in the rough, the clubface's grooves cannot grip the ball and apply backspin. Consequently, when the ball lands there is no braking effect. The cure requires understanding that this occurs and then adapting your technique accordingly.

TOUR CURE 41
ADAPT YOUR SHORT GAME STRATEGY AND TECHNIQUE

The cure for this problem is to adapt your target selection. Instead of looking at the flag, find a landing spot off the green in front of the pin. The idea is to land it and scrub off some speed to limit the amount of roll. If a bunker intrudes, as it did with Casey's shot (left), target a landing area away from the pin.

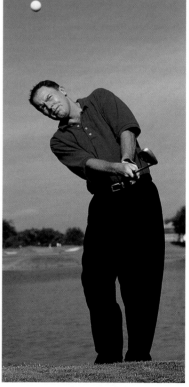

Adapting your technique also helps you put the ball on the green. Notice the clubface is facing the sky as the ball gains height, creating a higher, softer landing trajectory (photo above, right). A good way to accomplish this is to concentrate on having the knuckles of your left hand face the sky on a partial follow-through (photo at right), instead of facing the ground.

PRACTICE TEE

To hit successful shots out of the rough, you need to limit the amount of grass that gets between the clubface and the ball at impact. As Scott said, this is best accomplished by:

1 Playing the ball back farther in your stance.

2 Making your downswing descend instead of trying to sweep the ball out of the rough.

3 Remembering that sweeping traps the grass, but a descending approach limits the amount of grass that can get in between.

4 Realizing that your take-away is key.

BALL BACK IN STANCE

The ball is positioned back in my stance as I prepare to hit a 7-iron out of the rough. Even with this ball position, you can visualize a straight line down along my left arm and through the club shaft.

PICK UP THE CLUB

In Chapter 2, we emphasized starting your backswing with the shoulders. In the rough, we have to adapt the initial move away from the ball to encourage a descending swing path.

Picking up the club as the first order of movement will take it back along a steeper incline, setting a cocked wrist angle. From this position, you follow the same path back down and then accelerate through the ball.

Ball Flight,
Terrain
and
Rough
Cures:
Rough
Cures

4

SHORT GAME PROBLEMS

"Dear God, don't let me chili-dip this. Put it in the bunker if you want. Maybe I can hole it from the bunker." —Chi Chi Rodriguez *on hitting a wedge shot.*

As you get closer to the pin, technique, accuracy and distance control become the prime considerations. Eliminating problems affecting these factors sheds unwanted strokes from your game quickly.

Chi Chi Rodriguez and Fuzzy Zoeller—our two short game specialists— are here to correct pitching, chipping, bunker play and putting problems. Ben Hogan called Chi Chi the best bunker player he ever saw, and Fuzzy is a source for some outstanding chipping and putting help.

"I don't want anybody to know it, but I do practice." —Fuzzy Zoeller

IN THIS SECTION

PITCHING: SHORT APPROACH SHOTS

- Poor Target Selection

- Incorrect Setup to Create Loft

- Incorrect Swing Plane for Short Shots

- Lack of Distance Control

- Pitch and Run Stops too Early

- Practice Tee

BUNKER PROBLEMS

- No Feel in the Sand

- Level Lie Problems

- Downhill Problems

- Uphill Problems

- Fried Eggs

- Practice Tee

CHIPPING PROBLEMS

- Poor Address Position

- Poor Ball Position

- Stroke too Wristy

- Ball Never Finishes Close to the Hole

- Practice Tee

PUTTING PROBLEMS

- Incorrect Grip and Pressure

- Poor Posture and Eye Position

- Excessive Body Movement

- Flipping Wrists

- Poor Lag Putting

- Stroke too Inside or Outside

- Yips

- Speed is a Mystery

- Trouble with Reading the Line

- Practice Tee

PITCHING: SHORT APPROACH SHOTS

If you have problems with this phase of the game, Chi Chi can help. His solid and imaginative technique is simple to understand. Still playing competitive golf in his fifth decade on TOUR, he knows what your problems are and how to cure them.

The five cures covered in this section range from selecting the correct target to controlling your pitching distances. His objective: helping you stop the ball close to the pin! For outstanding drills to reinforce what Chi Chi says, visit Martin Hall on the Practice Tee.

PROBLEM 42
POOR TARGET SELECTION

The problem with poor target selection is that you probably don't realize you have a problem, as Patrick demonstrates in the photos below. He's pitching with a 9-iron and is focusing on the pin as his target. The results can be seen—the ball skipped through the green.

The only time you should make the pin your primary target is when hitting a high, soft shot with a lofted wedge. Before I help you work on your technique, let's cure your misconception about target selection.

Using the pin as your target will result in this: your ball skipping through the green.

TOUR CURE 42
TARGET WHERE YOU WANT TO LAND THE BALL

There are three keys to pitching the ball close to the pin: (1) decide on the type of shot you want to hit; (2) choose the spot where you want to land the ball as your target; and (3) select the club to match that shot.

Part of the problem is that the short game is made up of both technique and feel. You can learn technique, but practice is the only way to develop feel.

Feel begins with visualization. My cure for poor target selection begins with looking at the photo below with two pins and various targets. This illustrates the landing areas for several types of shots and how the ball will react. The next time you pitch, visualize your shot trajectory and landing target based on how you want the ball to react.

VISUALIZE THESE LANDING TARGETS

• **Red:** Lob shot. The pin is your target for a high, soft lob shot. Club selection: L-wedge.

• **Yellow:** Medium trajectory pitch. The landing target is between eight and 10 feet in front of the hole on a path that will allow the ball to run a short distance after landing. Club selection: pitching or sand wedge, depending on distance.

• **White:** Pitch-and-run. You would not play this shot to the right pin because of the bunker. You can play it to the left pin, and the landing target should be on the fringe or fairway in front of the green. This scrubs off some of the speed before the ball rolls toward the pin. Club selection: 8- or 9-iron, depending on the distance.

Short
Game
Problems:
Pitching:
Short
Approach
Shots

PROBLEM 43
INCORRECT SETUP

Setting up for shorter shots can be confusing because it varies from the long game. If your setup looks similar to Patrick's, you have several problems I need to correct. Let's begin on the ground and work our way up.

Problem: Grip too strong. The grip is perfect for hitting a draw off the tee, but a problem for hitting a higher, shorter shot.

Problem: No flex in knees. This rigid, upright stance will lead to a thin, topped shot, which is the opposite of the desired high, soft shot.

Problem: Hooded clubhead. This decreases the loft needed for a higher trajectory shot. Hooding or closing the club takes the bounce out of a wedge, increasing your risk of chili-dipping it or sculling the ball over the green.

Problem: Hands back. Thinking he needs to help the ball into the air, Patrick's hands are back, laying the club open so he can shovel the ball into the air.

Problem: Width of stance and alignment. This stance is too wide and the feet are parallel to the target line. This makes it difficult for the hips to clear on a shorter shot. An open clubface and an alignment parallel to the target line will send the ball off target to the right.

TOUR CURE 43
A SETUP FOR LOFT

Comparing my address position with the photo on the left page clearly illustrates the cures to your setup problems. Notice how a pitching setup differs from the one used for your longer game.

I do not have to hit the ball over 250 yards for this shot. My goal is laser-like accuracy along a chosen trajectory to hit my landing target.

Cure: My grip's V's point to the center. This is a neutral grip. Patrick's strong grip incorrectly results in the hands turning over and a lower, hotter shot. My neutral grip allows me to maintain the clubface angle through impact and launch a high shot with spin. For a higher lob wedge, I would weaken the grip by pointing the V's more toward the left.

Cure: Narrow stance. This is a feel shot that does not require a lot of lower body movement. Weight is preset on my left side because the shorter swing does not provide the time for a weight transfer back and forth. Open stance points left of your target, allowing you to swing your open clubface through the shot and have it square to the target line at impact.

Cure: Hands preset. I always preset everything. This is the position you want to return to at impact.

Cure: Flex in knees. Golf is an athletic sport. I set up with flexed knees to help absorb upper body movement.

Cure: *Square the clubface to the target line and open your stance. This adjusts the loft as needed for the higher trajectory. The more you open the face the higher the ball will go and the less distance it will travel.*

Short
Game
Problems:
Pitching:
Short
Approach
Shots

PROBLEM 44
TALL, UNFLEXED STANCE EQUALS INSIDE SWING

A pitch shot must get you close to the pin. Good pitchers follow a precise swing plane to impact the ball with a square clubface at the proper loft angle. Pitching accuracy is related to the address position.

Patrick has seen many of his students try to pitch with the low inside swing he's demonstrating as a result of being too tall at address.

INSIDE SWING PLANE: DESTROYS LOFT AND ACCURACY

This is the most common problem I see. The clubhead is only briefly on plane. Look at your wedge and notice how upright it is. An upright club is swung on an upright plane, not a shallow, inside plane.

TOUR CURE 44
UPRIGHT SWING PLANE

The goal of my swing plane is to return a square clubhead back to the ball with the additional loft I added at setup. This is the only way to produce an accurate, higher-trajectory shot that reaches your landing target. Here are my cures for swing plane problems.

1 - TAKE-AWAY

I begin by making a slow shoulder take-away from the ball. Notice my lower body has not moved, and the straight line that goes down my left arm through the shaft.

2 - STEEPER BACKSWING

My backswing brings the club back to a steeper position. The shaft of the wedge is shorter and more upright than longer irons and woods. You stand closer to the ball, so the club is swung more upright. Notice the shorter 9 o'clock backswing with the toe pointed toward the target.

3 - IMPACT DUPLICATES SETUP

This impact photo was taken at 1/8000 of a second and shows the clubhead just starting to slip under the ball. The important thing to notice, however, is the almost exact duplication of the impact (big photo) and setup (small inset photo) positions. The only differences are the slightly cleared hips and the flexed shaft ready to release, at impact.

4 - FOLLOW-THROUGH

Do not try to keep the clubhead square to the target line through follow-through. Notice how my clubhead correctly continues along the swing arc that takes it back to the inside following impact.

5 - FINISH POSITION

I finish facing the target. The length of my follow-through matches the length of my backswing—the subject of the next cure for distance control.

Short
Game
Problems:
Pitching:
Short
Approach
Shots

119

PROBLEM 45
DISTANCE CONTROL PROBLEMS

All feel shots require tempo and timing. This provides a balance and harmony to your movements. Patrick is demonstrating a problem that makes it difficult to control your pitching distance.

He made a short backswing and a high follow-through. Instead of being smooth through impact, he is fast and jerky. The ball stays low and will overshoot the green because his energy went into producing a lifting motion, which lacks tempo, timing and feel.

ADDITIONAL DISTANCE CONTROL PROBLEMS

- Failure to select the correct landing target for the type of shot played.

- Choosing the wrong club loft for the shot.

- Incorrect positions at setup.

A short backswing (left) and high follow-through (right) will send your ball low and probably make it overshoot the green.

TOUR CURE 45
MIRROR IMAGE

I have two cures to help you control the distances you hit your pitch shots. The first I can demonstrate, but the second you have to learn on your own.

First, you have to match your backswing and follow-through. Second, you must practice your feel. Everything isn't cut-and-dried in golf, and just practicing good distance control, getting a good feel, is a good remedy to go with matching your backswing and follow-through.

MIRROR IMAGE

My 9 o'clock backswing (left) and 3 o'clock follow-through (right) match. This helps create the tempo and timing needed to control the distance of my pitch shots. Practice is the only way I can learn how far my shots go.

Short
Game
Problems:
Pitching:
Short
Approach
Shots

PROBLEM 46
PITCH-AND-RUN STOPS EARLY

Patrick demonstrates just why his pitch and run will not release after landing. Notice how steep he is swinging down on the ball. This type of extreme downward motion creates loads of backspin, which is wonderful for stopping the ball, but deadly if you want it to run.

The temptation is to hit down even harder, but this only increases the backspin. In my cure, I'll show you how to properly play this mini-swing shot so your ball releases and rolls to the hole after landing.

Extreme downward motion creates too much backspin, which may stop your ball too early.

TOUR CURE 46
PITCH-AND-RUN: PLAY BALL BACK AND SHALLOW YOUR SWING PATH

A pitch-and-run shot is a wonderful alternative for hitting a high lob shot at the pin. The key to this shot is to land your ball on an interim target along the path to the hole, then let the ball run the rest of the distance to the pin.

With the development of the lob wedge, certain pitch-and-run shots have become a forgotten art. But they are potent, effective shots to have in your arsenal. Here is a photo sequence showing how I hit mine.

PLAYING BACK AND SHALLOW

I hit a pitch-and-run with a less-lofted club. Instead of a wedge, choose an 8-iron and bounce the ball up. I take a last look at the target (1) to program my mind for the distance to the landing area. With the ball positioned off my back foot and after I have choked down on the club, I make a shallow, lower backswing (2). The length depends on the distance. As I start down to the ball (3), the shoulders do the work since this is an upper body swing. The clubhead returns to the ball (4) and you can see how I replicate my setup position here at impact. The follow-through length (5) mirrors the backswing. The ball is lower, and will release and run after landing.

Short
Game
Problems:
Pitching:
Short
Approach
Shots

PRACTICE TEE

Good short game players have good vision. They can see the shot before they hit it. Unfortunately, those with short game problems really have no idea where to land the ball.

I believe the best way to begin curing your pitching problems is to help develop a mental image of throwing a ball at a target. My own preference is to land a ball on the green as soon as possible, as long as the green is flat. I don't suggest landing the ball into either an uphill or downhill slope.

BALL TOSS DRILL

I remember Mark O'Meara telling me about the countless hours he spent with Greg Norman tossing balls around the green. Throwing a ball at a target is easier to visualize than pitching a ball at a target.

In this series of photos, I'm throwing a golf ball underhanded and asking myself:

1 What trajectory did the ball fly on?

2 Where did it land?

3 How much did it roll after landing?

The target also depends on the topography of the green.

Just throwing balls and watching how they fly, land and roll is good practice for helping you visualize when you're going to pitch during a real round.

MARTIN'S CLUB SELECTIONS

How do you know which club to use? That depends on how far off the green you are and how deep into the green the flag is. Because I like to land the ball on the green as soon as possible, here is my formula:

• If the distance between you and the pin is 60-percent fairway and 40-percent green, I would use a sand wedge. The ball carries 60 percent and rolls 40 percent.

• If the distance relationship changed to 50/50, I would choose a pitching wedge.

• If the relationship was 40-percent carry and 60-percent roll, I would pitch with a 9-iron. This occurs when you are not that far off the green and the pin is set back.

BACKSWING RACQUET DRILL

The biggest reason the club must be on plane for pitching is that when your club is on the correct plane, the bottom of the swing arc tends to be in the correct place—where the ball is!

The more the club gets off plane, the harder it is to get to the bottom of the arc, and that's where you get the mis-hits from. Holding a badminton racquet along the shaft provides a visual understanding of clubface position.

Set up with the badminton racquet facing your target.

At the top of your backswing—which for pitching is usually the 9 o'clock position with the shaft vertical—the racquet should be opened and parallel to your target line. Notice the toe of the club points toward the target.

Wrong

If the racquet is in this closed position, you probably have been hitting balls to the left.

DROP ARM FOR DISTANCE CONTROL DRILL

Over-accelerating the hands and arms from the top of the backswing down and through impact hits the ball too far, but trying to slow down hits it too short.

How much should your arms accelerate downward? Try this drill to develop the feeling.

• Raise your arms so they are parallel to the ground.

• Let them drop naturally and allow gravity to demonstrate the feel.

• This is the motion you want to feel from your arms.

• The distance you hit the ball is determined by how much backswing you make and by the natural feeling of the arms falling from that point.

Drop your arms from horizontal to get the feel of how fast they should accelerate downward on a pitch.

Short
Game
Problems:
Pitching:
Short
Approach
Shots

EVEN ACCELERATION DRILL

Pitching is different from your long game swings, as you've seen both from the cures Chi Chi suggested, and from these Practice Tee drills. You don't want to rapidly accelerate the downswing, as you would for the long game. Smoothness is the key to distance control. You must match your backswing and follow-through lengths.

Here are three sets of matched swings using only my left arm to develop feel. Increasing the backswing and matching it on the follow-through develops additional distance. Think of this in terms of a clock face.

9 TO 3

10 TO 2

11 TO 1

BUNKER PROBLEMS

Golf course architects seem to save their special creativity for bunker design. The many shapes, sizes and depths attract the eye as well as the ball of even the best golfers.

Landing in the sand can be a positive thing once you understand the technique needed to stop the ball close to the pin. With the exceptions of buried lies or being trapped under the lip, bunker play should not deter you from shooting a good score.

Chi Chi is the man to help solve your bunker problems. Regardless of the lie, he has the cure. And Martin Hall has the drills on the Practice Tee.

PROBLEM 47
NO FEEL IN THE SAND

Bunker problems got you down? Most bunker problems are related to not understanding what sand play is all about. A fat or thinned shot is the usual unsatisfactory result. Begin correcting your problems by developing a positive attitude, where you think about holing a bunker shot instead of just getting out of the bunker.

TOUR CURE 47
BASIC TRAINING

My four-step program to bunker basics starts the process of curing your problems. Let's start with implementing a "holing out, not just getting out" strategy, followed by some basics for improving your sand play.

Your landing target should always be four feet short of the hole, regardless of the lie. If the ball rolls three feet or five feet after landing, you have a tap-in.

STEP 1: LAND FOUR FEET SHORT OF THE HOLE

STEP 2: OPEN CLUBFACE AND STANCE

- The speed of the club and how much you open or close the clubface controls bunker shot distances.

- Always make clubface adjustments before gripping so you can return the clubface exactly this way at impact.

- The open clubface should be squared to the target line but your foot line must be open and aimed left of the target. Weight is always on the left foot—shifting weight in the sand causes a loss of balance.

- Swing along your foot line.

STEP 3: ADJUST THE RIGHT HAND

- Weaken the grip by shifting the left hand V more to the left of your body.

- Weakening adds loft because the clubface stays open through impact.

STEP 4: ENTER AND EXIT

With high-speed photography, notice the club entering the sand behind the ball. As a result, a sand cushion is developing to propel the ball out of the bunker.

As the swing continues, the clubhead along the foot line path is clearly visible as the ball continues to climb and fly toward the pin.

PROBLEM 48
LEVEL LIE PROBLEMS

Normally, the ball is propelled by the clubface making direct contact, but bunker play calls for a different approach. The sand propelling the ball up and out is hard for some golfers to adapt to.

Patrick is watching his ball slam into the bunker face. In this case, the clubhead hit the ball, presenting him with the unwanted opportunity of trying

to get out again. Had the bunker face not stopped it, the ball would have sculled over the green.

Cure this problem by changing your bunker technique to one that can consistently create a narrow cut of sand to propel the ball. In some cases, this requires a steeper downswing. For a level lie, my cure shows how to approach it.

When trying to get out of a bunker, you don't want the clubhead hitting the ball.

TOUR CURE 48
CREATING A NARROW CUT OF SAND

Stay in control instead of flailing away at the ball. A smooth, rhythmic swing is your best ally. Create tempo and timing and your problem is almost cured.

The swing arrow below shows the difference in a bunker shot compared to a regular shot. Normally, the club comes from inside the target line, squares at impact and then goes back inside. A bunker shot, especially a short one, goes outside, squares at impact and goes outside again. It's a semicircle away from your body.

Instead of taking a huge sand divot, concentrate on slipping an open clubface into the sand several ball lengths behind your ball. The open face passing underneath builds a narrow cut of sand to propel it out. A good follow-through completes the package.

Notice the narrow cut of sand propelling the ball. The distance of the shot is controlled by the speed of your rotation down to the ball, and by how open or closed the clubface is.

Following through and facing the target at the finish are imperative for a smooth, rhythmic swing.

Short
Game
Problems:
Bunker
Problems

PROBLEM 49
DOWNHILL PROBLEMS

Trying to help the ball into the air off a downhill bunker lie is courting disaster. Patrick tried to utilize the level shot technique for this downhill shot with the unfortunate result of bouncing the club directly into the ball. Avoid the temptation to help lift balls into the air on a downslope.

In golf, you get into trouble by trying to help the ball into the air with your swing. Clubs are manufactured with loft, which provides all the lift needed if the shot is executed correctly.

In this situation, the key is to adapt the path of your downswing to the lie. In this downhill example, it needs to be steeper to increase the amount of sand necessary to lift and send the ball out of the bunker.

Here are some other problems I see in Patrick's setup:

The ball position is forward when it should be back in the stance. His hands are not in the preset forward impact position. Patrick's shoulders are tilted, not level, and his weight is on the right foot instead of the left.

TOUR
Cures

132

TOUR CURE 49
DOWNHILL SWING ADJUSTMENT

WEIGHT ON LEFT LEG, BALL BACK

SWING DOWN

Hitting down more on the ball, from the top to where the club enters the sand, will bring the face under the ball. Clubface loft can then go to work, building the sand cushion needed to propel the ball out of the bunker.

BIGGER CUSHION OF SAND

Compare the amount of sand in this photo and the level-lie photo (page 131). A larger sand cushion is needed to get the ball airborne from the downhill lie. My adjustments enabled me to stay down with the ball.

For a downhill bunker lie, I put my weight on my left leg, position the ball back in my stance and swing more down on it. This makes it much easier to stay down with the shot and get the club under the ball. The key is to begin your swing by picking the club up to encourage a steeper backswing.

Short
Game
Problems:
Bunker
Problems

133

PROBLEM 50
UPHILL PROBLEMS

Patrick is really having trouble with this shot. It's going to get out, but his next shot will be a chip instead of a putt. That's a wasted stroke.

Once again, setup was to blame. Trying to get balance into the shot, his weight is incorrectly on his right foot when it should be on the left. Always place more weight on the left foot in sand.

The next problem is his head position. I know a lot of instructors teach that the head should be behind the ball, which is the position he has here. But I have a different opinion. The head should be on line with the ball or slightly ahead.

Patrick's hand position is another problem. Hands back in the stance are the telltale sign of a "helper upper." Always preset your hands forward of the ball in the impact position.

Too much weight on the right leg. Poor head position. Hands back in the stance. This shot produced the need for a chip shot rather than a putt, costing a stroke.

TOUR CURE 50
BUILD FORWARD BALANCE

My uphill setup, compared with Patrick's, shows a more balanced position to execute the shot. My head is on line with the ball and my weight is forward. I angled my feet into a stance that provides a stable platform to hit off.

My hands are forward in the preset impact position. The clubface is aimed at the pin, but my feet are open. All I need to do is make a swing that follows my foot line, as you can see by the swing path through the sand in the large photo.

Angled feet make a stable platform.

Balanced position.

PROBLEM 51
FRIED EGGS

A high, lofted shot that misses the green and lands in the bunker can become plugged. The ball is partially buried in the sand, looking like the yolk in an egg fried sunny-side up.

The more common situation is a lower shot that plugs on the uphill face of a bunker. Patrick's efforts only moved the ball slightly from this position, freeing it from its plugged lie, but he wasted a stroke. Hooding the club and leaving it in the ground did not have the effect he hoped for.

Did you think that every lie you get in golf is going to be a good one? This is a tough shot for even a highly skilled golfer because of the uncertainty of what the ball will do when it comes out.

There are some things you can do to improve your chances for making a good shot.

Patrick unburied the fried egg (left), but he's going to need another stroke to get completely out of the bunker (right). Chi Chi's recipe for fried eggs is on the next page.

TOUR CURE 51
DELIVERING THE FRIED EGG

I'm holding a pitching wedge, which is part of the cure for this problem. It is very hard to get a sand wedge under a buried ball because a sand wedge has more bounce than any other club.

I open a pitching wedge, instead of hooding it, before taking my grip.

CHI CHI'S FRIED EGG SUGGESTIONS

- Downhill fried eggs: Close the face. You may take the chance of going 30 feet past the hole and have to rely on your putting, but you got out.

- Flat lie fried egg: You want to stop the ball fast after landing. Use the pitching wedge to dig the club under the ball and follow through.

- Back pin: With a lot of distance to the pin, you want the ball to run. Slightly close the clubface and dig the club under the ball. The decreased clubface loft and your follow-through increase the roll after landing.

IMPACT

I pick the club straight up in the air and come straight down. The face stays open as it digs under the ball. I'm swinging along my foot line. The open clubface is propelling the ball up and slightly right toward the pin.

HIGH AND SOFT

I didn't consciously leave the club in the ground. The sand absorbs all the energy and keeps it there. The ball is on a high, soft trajectory from a very difficult lie because the face stays open through impact.

Short Game Problems: Bunker Problems

137

PRACTICE TEE

The biggest mistake most golfers make with bunker play is getting the bottom of their swing arc too far behind the ball. They take plenty of sand, but the club is on the way up when it impacts the ball, blading it across the green.

The lowest point of the swing arc must be under the ball. It's like the ball has a pair of legs and you're trying to chop them off. Here's a list of what you need to hit this shot properly. The lines in the sand will help you execute the shot:

- Stance open.
- Ball forward.
- Grip weak.
- Feel as if you are cutting across the shot.
- Have plenty of turn in your follow-through.

SAND DIAGRAM DRILL

I drew some lines in the sand to diagram the entire sand shot. You should do the same. The straight arrow is the target line. I also placed a line by my feet and drew an arc that leaves the target line and parallels my foot line. This is the line the club swings along as it cuts under the ball. Notice the open clubface points straight down the target line.

SWING FOLLOWS THE DIAGRAM

My backswing parallels the target line and my follow-through past impact shows the club followed a line that paralleled my foot line. This puts a slice spin on the ball and it stops soon after landing. Draw this diagram when you practice.

FRIED EGG TEE DRILL

With a fried egg, you can't really get under this ball to any great degree, so we have to shovel the ball forward. I'm going to place a tee under the ball. The point of this drill is to shovel the tee out of the ground.

1 Place a tee in your sand diagram at the point where the ball would be positioned.

2 Place the ball on a tee.

3 Slightly close the clubface and position the ball back in your stance. Make sure your weight is forward. The objective of my downswing will be to pinch the ball at impact.

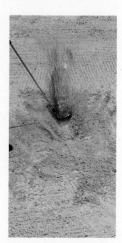

4 The club digs down and shovels the tee and ball forward.

CHIPPING
PROBLEMS

How can such a short stroke cause so many problems? All players can be good chippers and consistently get the ball close. In fact, with a few tips and some cures, you can develop a professional's chipping game!

Driving the ball 300 yards is not a reasonable objective for most members, but holing a chip shot is well within your ability, or it will be after Fuzzy Zoeller fixes a few things.

Combine Martin Hall's one-arm drills on the Practice Tee with Fuzzy's tips and watch your scores drop lower.

PROBLEM 52
ADDRESS POSITION

Good chippers repeat their accurate strokes time and time again because they set up for success. Inconsistent chippers set themselves up in some pretty imaginative ways.

Everybody gets lucky once in awhile and holes a chip, but you need a permanent solution to your problem. Let's look at Patrick as he demonstrates the most common of all the amateur address positions.

The overall impression is that this is a non-professional setup. Weight is incorrectly on the right side and away from the target and posture is too upright. In addition, he's holding the club too high on the grip. The hands should not be behind the ball and the feet should not be parallel to the target line.

TOUR CURE 52
PROFESSIONAL ADDRESS

Every time I chip the ball I know I can hole the shot. I don't always do it, of course, but if I have the correct line and speed, the ball will go in. I play this game professionally and take chipping very seriously. I must deliver the ball on the line to the hole each time I chip.

My posture differs in some very important elements from Patrick's. Compare the two as I point out the corrections to his—and possibly your—address problems.

This position looks far less complicated than Patrick's. Most of the weight is on my left side and toward the target. My posture is slightly more compact and flexed. Notice the good spine angle. I choke down on the club and my hands are forward of the ball, pre-setting the impact position. The clubface points straight at the line the ball will roll on and my stance is open.

PROBLEM 53
POOR BALL POSITION

Patrick is demonstrating what happens when the ball is not correctly positioned in the stance. Some instructors say if you want to hit a high, lofted chip, put the ball up in your stance. But when less-skilled players have the ball up in their stance, they incorrectly try to help the ball into the air with their club.

Off-line and wrong trajectory shots can be attributed to ball position, and to the quality of your stroke. Now that you corrected your posture problems, we need to work on ball position and movement.

TOUR CURE 53
CENTER BALL POSITION

The center ball position lets you maintain the same posture and the same ball position. You only need to change your club to take care of the varying distances. This chipping approach works especially well for golfers whose schedules do not permit hours of practice.

I think all chips can be hit from the center of the stance. With this constant position, you can hit the flop shot and the low shot.

CHANGE CLUBS, NOT BALL POSITION

Develop a consistent chipping posture and ball position, then use it every time. The only variable: the club you choose.

Short
Game
Problems:
Chipping
Problems

141

PROBLEM 54
WRISTY STROKE

How many times do you hear the terms *tempo* and *timing* associated with golf? The answer is *always*, because tempo and timing affect every stroke. Watch a professional chip and you see us take the club back and then bring it forward. Notice I left out the word *swing*.

Patrick is *swinging* at his chip shot. When you think of a swing, you think of releasing the wrists or flipping them, as he's doing in this case. The key to good, crisp chipping is to maintain firm wrists.

Notice how Patrick's wrists are collapsing through impact. The reason: He is trying to help the ball into the air! Club manufacturers do an excellent job of building loft into their clubs. Let the club do the work, not your wrists.

Flipping wrists are the problem with this chip. Firm wrists through impact are key to good, crisp chip shots.

TOUR CURE 54
FIRM WRISTS THROUGH IMPACT

The club only moves a few feet when you chip. Martin Hall has a great drill at the end of this chapter to develop the proper angle for the club-head to approach the ball on the downswing. My job is to correct your wrist problem.

Study all four of these photos, paying close attention to my wrists. Did they flip through the shot or did the back of my left wrist remain firm? It remained firm! A great drill, if I can intrude on Martin's turf for a moment, is to put a ruler in your watchband and chip. This keeps your left wrist firm.

Short
Game
Problems:
Chipping
Problems

143

PROBLEM 55
BALL SELDOM FINISHES CLOSE TO HOLE

If your ball seldom finishes close to the hole, you may think that holing a chip is nothing more than a pipe dream. Poor accuracy is a result of bad posture, poor ball position or wristy stroke, but we've already cured these.

The only remaining reason for not finishing close to the hole may be a misunderstanding as to what a chip shot really is. Chipping is a way to fly the ball over grass that may knock your ball off course if it had to roll through it. Chip shot trajectories stay close to the ground and ideally the ball should land just on the green and roll the rest of the way to the hole. Correct club selection takes care of the distance.

Patrick hit a lofted shot to a far pin and ended way short, since the ball did not release after landing. A better choice would have been to take a 9-iron, land the ball just on the green, and let it run the rest of the way to the hole.

Chip shots are not lofty, high-trajectory shots, as these photos show. Chip shots should stay low, land early and roll to the hole.

TOUR CURE 55
CLUB TAKES CARE OF THE DISTANCE

Once you cure the other problems in this chipping section, proper club selection will get you close every time. Occasionally, you will hole one and, as your confidence soars, strokes will begin dropping off your score.

The key is selecting the right club to cover the distance between you and the pin. All the courses I've played over the years seem to place their pins in a variety of locations, so you need to constantly decide on the appropriate club. My usual choices are shown in the photo on the right … a 9-iron, pitching wedge or sand wedge.

FUZZY'S CLUB SELECTION TIPS

After reading the putting line to the hole, I have to select the correct club for the various pin placements. The following list represents my choices from this position just off the green.

The only variable would be the firmness of the green. If the green is mushy, I would go with a less lofted club to give the chip more rolling power. Practice helps develop the feel for clubhead speed.

- **Center of the Green Pin:** Use a 52-degree wedge or pitching wedge. Land the ball two to three feet on the green and let it run the remaining 20 feet to the hole.

- **Far Pin Placement:** Use a 9-iron or pitching wedge. Land the ball quickly on the green. Less loft than a wedge allows the ball to roll a longer distance.

- **Close Pin Placement:** Use a pitching wedge. Land the ball just on the green and the greater loft will limit the roll to the hole.

Short
Game
Problems:
Chipping
Problems

145

Improving your short game lowers your score quickly. Many shots are wasted from very close to the hole. Here on the Practice Tee, I'm going to demonstrate some drills to help you maximize the information Fuzzy provided in this chapter. We begin with ball position and your nose!

NOSE AHEAD OF BALL

The purpose of this drill is to eliminate the common setup problems we saw Patrick demonstrate in Problem 48: head behind the ball with the left shoulder high. If you hit behind the ball, this position is responsible for bottoming out the swing arc too soon. To illustrate, I'm using a whiffle ball on a rope.

CORRECT POSITION

INCORRECT POSITION

The hanging ball shows the golf ball is behind my nose. This ensures that my weight will primarily be on the left foot, and the left shoulder will not be high. The reason: The chipping downward movement is from high to low, and a high left shoulder would cause it to incorrectly go low to high.

The golf ball is ahead of my nose and my left shoulder is high. This is not correct and I will be unable to chip with a high to low movement.

ONE-ARM DRILL NO. 1

This practice drill helps you understand the need to feel pressure in the last three fingers of the left hand (small photo at right). Also, place your right hand in your left armpit and keep it pressed against your chest with a little pressure from your left upper arm.

As you swing, you will notice you must have a little pivot from your feet, knees and shoulders to chip. Small swings require small pivots. You can't just brush the club back with your arms. Concentrate on maintaining a firm left wrist through the swing.

ONE-ARM DRILL NO. 2

As I set up for this right-handed swinging drill, I use the four fingers of my left hand as a bridge between the shaft and the right forearm. This maintains a little pressure from my right arm against the fingers of my left hand.

Keeping that pressure constant while making my swing ensures that the right wrist angle does not change during the stroke. I'm not adding or reducing my wrist action.

How to grip the club.

Constant pressure means the angle of your right wrist stays the same throughout the stroke.

Short
Game
Problems:
Chipping
Problems

HIGH-TO-LOW DRILL

Place the grip of another club six to seven inches behind the ball. The key to this drill is to bring the club down over that grip without touching it to chip the ball. Practice using this drill and you will quickly develop the proper downward motion.

MARTIN'S CLUB SELECTION FORMULA

This table is a good starting point to choose the correct club for chipping. But you need to adjust your selections for faster or slower greens and the quality of your lie.

• **5-iron:** Will give you one part carry and five parts roll. If you are 10 feet off the green and the pin is 50 feet on the green, the 5-iron is the correct club.

• **7-iron:** Will give you one part carry and three parts roll. If you are 10 feet off the green and the flag is 30 feet back, the 7-iron is the correct club.

• **9-iron:** One part carry and two parts roll. You can do the math!

• **Sand wedge:** One part carry and one part roll.

PUTTING PROBLEMS

Bobby Jones once criticized Sam Snead's sidesaddle putting style. But the Slammer had a great comeback: "Well, Bob, when you come in off the course they don't ask you how, they ask you how many."

There is more room for diversity in putting style than in any other phase of the game. As Fuzzy points out in this chapter, you need to have a style that is comfortable for *you*. Of course, it has to provide repeatable success too.

That's where Fuzzy comes in. He wants to help you, but makes it clear that his style is different from most. He had to adapt for his peripheral vision but, as his record shows, your style does not have to be textbook to be successful. All you need is a square putter face at impact.

Fuzzy has the cures here. Martin Hall's Practice Tee drills provide additional help for building an excellent putting stroke.

PROBLEM 56
INCORRECT GRIP AND TENSION

Good putters use a pull-and-push movement to roll the ball accurately along a visualized target line to the hole. A pendulum motion is a good way to describe it.

A balanced grip, with the palms facing each other, encourages this motion. They form a solid unit: The arms and shoulders work harmoniously together, rocking back and through the stroke.

Patrick is demonstrating grips that fight that process. While putting is a highly individual part of the game, these grips will not allow the stroke to produce consistent results. Members with unbalanced grips occasionally make a good putt but then hopelessly spend the rest of their round trying to recapture the magic.

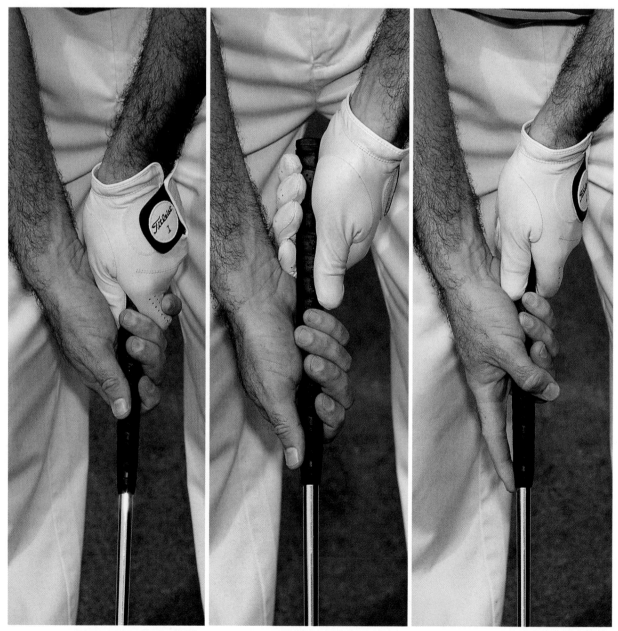

These three unbalanced grips make for inaccurate, inconsistent putting.

TOUR CURE 56
BALANCED AND LIGHT GRIP

Looking at my grip you see lots of fingers, but also notice two other things: the ball is going into the hole and my palms are facing each other. I was taught the pull-push stroke, which takes the putter back with the left hand and hits it with the right. My grip is balanced—a great cure for those poor grips seen on the previous page.

I only place four fingers of my left hand on the club. My thumb is short on the grip to provide additional control. The index finger will overlap. Notice how the wide part of the grip fits against my palm.

The palm of the right hand fits on the opposite side of the grip and, when closed, the left index finger overlaps.

Good putters feel the putter head during the stroke. Carbite and other manufacturers have developed putters with great balance. Light tension and a balanced grip develops a good working relationship.

Grip your club lightly so someone can pull it out of your fingers. The lighter your grip, the lighter the touch you have in your fingers.

Short
Game
Problems:
Putting
Problems

151

PROBLEM 57
POOR POSTURE AND EYE POSITION

While it's okay to express some individuality in your putting setup, Patrick is demonstrating two obvious problems that won't develop the consistency you need to be a good putter: (1) his eyes are outside the target line; and (2) his hands are back of the ball.

I want you to understand that everybody is different. Allen Doyle uses a flat putter, as does Hubert Green, and their posture is bent over at address.

Experiment to find what feels comfortable for you. You play this game the way you feel, and if you don't feel comfortable, you won't play well. One hard rule is that your eyes should be over or inside the target and your hands should be in front of the ball.

Two problems here: Eyes outside the target line (left), and hands back of the ball (right).

TOUR CURE 57
BE COMFORTABLE AND ATHLETIC

Peripheral vision means more to me than posture. I have very shallow peripheral vision. If I stand over a putt with my eyes over the ball, as most instruction books say, I can't see down the line.

To compensate for this, I flattened my putter four or five degrees so I can get back away from the ball. My eyes are more inside than suggested by others, as the hanging club shows.

I see better and can shoot the ball down the line. The cure for eye alignment is to position them either over or slightly inside the ball, but never outside.

FUZZY'S ADDRESS POSITION

- Putter aimed at starting point of line to the hole.

- Open stance.

- Ball positioned back in stance.

- Flexed knees.

- Facing palms.

- Solid hands, arms and shoulders move as a unit.

- Firm left wrist.

- Slight right wrist angle.

- Hands ahead of ball.

PROBLEM 58
EXCESSIVE BODY MOVEMENT/WRIST FLIPPING

Patrick is demonstrating problems he sees when giving lessons at Bay Hill. Instead of a smooth pull-and-push stroke that delivers a square clubface to the ball, notice the excessive body motion and flipping wrists.

As you look at these examples, what would you say Patrick's chances are for consistently sending the ball in a specific direction? Slim and none may be too generous!

A squared blade at impact allows the ball to smoothly roll along your putting path without spinning off the line. This gives the ball a chance to go in the hole or leave you with a short tap-in.

Throw in all the excess body movement and wrist flipping, and a reasonable goal would be a three-putt. How many strokes can you save if you two-putt instead of three-putt?

Too much body motion (left) and flipping wrists (right) make for poor putting.

TOUR CURE 58
MAINTAIN THE ANGLES

I think a lot of golfers are over-taught. They try to do too many things by the book instead of allowing their instincts to take over. The putting stroke is an excellent example.

The pendulum stroke cures the motion we just saw. But in all honesty, I'm more of a hands-type player than a shoulder-type. I think the quickest way to get through to your brain is through the fingers.

The photos below show the pendulum motion alongside my swing. The differences are subtle but they share a common similarity: I maintain the same right wrist angle during both. To develop the pendulum stroke, I sometimes use the Putterball training club across my chest and under my upper arms. This keeps the unit together.

BACKSWING

IMPACT

FOLLOW-THROUGH

Short
Game
Problems:
Putting
Problems

155

PROBLEM 59
POOR DISTANCE CONTROL

Sometimes you putt the ball well past the hole, while other times it stops well short. This is a problem that does not give you a clue to the cause.

A lack of confidence is the problem. This comes about as a result of how most golfers practice putting. I can walk on any practice putting green and watch amateurs practicing 40- or 50-footers, but rarely the money putts from within six feet.

Your brain is a computer and it learns from the information you feed it. Nothing makes the brain work more efficiently than success—watching the ball go into the hole. But how many of those 40- and 50-footers do you sink?

Watch us practice on the putting green. Do you see Phil Mickelson putting clear across the green to some distant hole, or is he trying to sink 100 putts in a row from three feet? By the way, if he misses, he begins all over again. My confidence cure is coming up.

Practicing unlikely putts breeds little confidence. Never seeing the ball go into the hole isn't good! Get closer, have success, then move on back.

TOUR CURE 59
LISTEN TO THE BALL GOING INTO THE HOLE

Before every round, professionals program their minds for success. We work on only our money putts from between three and six feet. We want every one of those putts to go in. Nothing breeds putting confidence faster than the sound of the ball plopping into the cup.

When you know and feel you can make these shorter putts, your confidence also grows when faced with a long one. You can be more aggressive on that long putt because your confidence is high for making the shorter one if you miss. Trust me, a lot of good things happen from long range when you know the next one is going in. Practice like a pro, as I'm doing in the photos.

START CLOSE AND MOVE BACK

Practice from close-in and start sinking those putts all the time. Then move back a little.

FUZZY'S LONG PUTT PHILOSOPHY

Knowing you can make the short putts helps cure the long putt distance control problem—be aggressive and go for it. It's better to be a little long than short if you plan on holing these. Good long putters are outstanding short putters!

PROBLEM 60
INSIDE/OUT AND OUTSIDE/IN STROKES

I love this Putterball that Carbite makes because it's a ball hitting a ball and there's no margin for error. If you are not square to the putting line at impact, the ball immediately leaves the correct putting path.

Putterball provides the instant feedback to help develop a square blade at impact. Martin Hall's Practice Tee drills quickly help you build a stroke that brings the club to the ball square every time. Some drills are as simple as clapping your hands.

INSIDE/OUT PATH

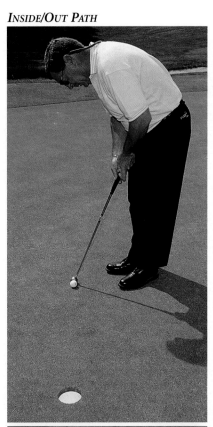

OUTSIDE/IN PATH

Using the Putterball, see how this inside/out swing path deflected the ball to the left of the hole. In this case, the Putterball hit the off-center outside portion of the ball. Had it hit the off-center inside portion, the ball would have spun to the right.

This outside/in stroke hit the off-center outside portion and sent the ball to the left. Had it impacted on the off-center inside portion, the ball would have spun right. Putting requires precision to ensure your putter blade is square to the ball at impact, preventing these off-line shots.

TOUR CURE 60
SQUARE THE BLADE AT IMPACT

See, the ball will go into the hole if your stroke brings the Putterball back square to the ball. Your putting stroke must have this same motion.

CLUBHEAD PATH

We created this photo to show the path my clubhead takes during the stroke.

- I'm more of a flare putter, using my left hand to take it back.

- The putter opens a little on the backswing.

- The clubhead squares to the putting line at impact.

- I use my right hand to stroke back and hit the ball.

- Do not take the putter head back straight or follow-through straight.

- Remember the club-under-the-arm drill created a small arc.

Problem 61
Downhill and Uphill Curvature Problems

Bless Patrick's heart. He is such a good golfer and teacher and yet he is portraying a man of all problems! In this case, he shows the usual outcome of breaking uphill and downhill putts.

Seldom does an uphill-breaking putt finish long and above the hole, and almost never do downhill putts finish short and above the hole. One problem is seen in the small photo below. The ball is incorrectly positioned the same for both when the physics need to be slightly different.

There is a very small difference in distance on a putting blade, but physics enters in and can either help or hurt you. Most putters have a center-line for aiming, but I want you to also use it to cure your uphill and downhill problems.

TOUR CURE 61
THE CLUBFACE HAS THREE PARTS

An older gentleman taught me when I was young that your putter is just a blade, but it helps on right-to-left or downhill putts to move the ball just beyond the centerline toward the toe.

Why is that? It helps keep the ball on line as opposed to pulling the ball to the left for a downhill putt. On left-to-right or uphill putts, I do the opposite and play the ball slightly on the heel side of the centerline.

That should help cure any problems you have with the distance and break. I make the same stroke for each and allow the position to compensate accordingly.

This works very well for me, but it may not work for you. Experiment and practice using different parts of the blade for different breaking situations.

TOWARD THE TOE FOR DOWNHILL PUTTS

TOWARD THE HEEL FOR UPHILL PUTTS

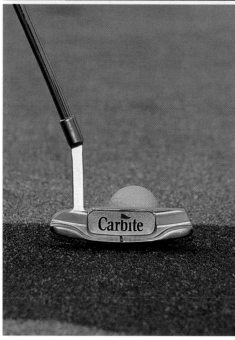

Downhill: toward the toe.

Uphill: toward the heel.

Short
Game
Problems:
Putting
Problems

161

PROBLEM 62
READING THE SPEED

The pace your putt takes to the hole is just as important as the line. Different speeds can produce different results along the same path. Patrick read the correct line to the hole but he forgot to check which way the grain was running. As a result, the ball finished short and off line.

You may think you misread the break when you actually misread the speed. Another problem is thinking the speed on the practice green will match the speed of the course's greens. That usually is not the case.

Do you want to know how a veteran like me assesses the speed when I walk onto the green? That's the essence of the cure for this problem.

Too much or too little speed can muck up what otherwise was a well-planned shot.

TOUR CURE 62
THE GRAIN AND NATURE'S WAY

Before setting foot on a green, I already know quite a bit about its speed. I'm not clairvoyant, but I do understand nature's role in golf. Every golf course has some dominant trait that affects speed.

Here at the TPC at River Highlands, home of the Canon Greater Hartford Open, there is a river that runs along the course. If you figure out how the course follows the river, you will find the greens always break toward the river. It acts as a gravity pull.

The direction the grass grows also affects the speed. Putting with the grain is faster than against it. If you play bermuda greens, the grain always grows in the direction of the setting sun. The exception is on an incline. In that case, the grain would grow with the flow of water going off the green.

Bentgrass greens do not have a lot of grain, so think of the speed in terms of how water would run off the green.

CHECK THE HOLE

Checking the hole reveals the direction the grain is growing. The smooth side of the cup is with the grain, while the rough side is against the grain.

This is a great drill to practice speed. I simply try to hit one ball with another, as I did here. I repeat this process all over the green to get a feeling for the speed. Notice that for this drill I'm focusing on hitting a ball, not the hole. For more drills, Martin Hall is waiting on the Practice Tee.

Short
Game
Problems:
Putting
Problems

PRACTICE TEE

The most important component to becoming a good putter is the clubface angle when it contacts the ball. It must be square if the ball is going to roll on line.

PIPE DRILL

A piece of PVC pipe will help you detect if the club-face is square at impact or if you have an open or closed problem.

To build a good stroke, the first thing you have to do is learn to control the face of the club. Practice making the pipe roll straight by using the next few drills.

Using a small piece of PVC pipe, I place some masking tape around it and a line down the center.

I line up my putter square at address.

If the pipe rolls straight, the clubface was square at impact. If it cartwheels to the left, the clubface was closed at impact. If it cartwheels to the right, the clubface was open at impact.

OPPOSING PALM DRILL

The clubface is really an extension of your right palm. Whatever the palm of your right hand does, the putter face follows. When you clap your hands, your palms have to strike squarely together to make any sound. This drill builds on that idea to help develop a square clubface at impact.

The putter face does what your right hand does.

At address, I hold my left hand on line with the PVC pipe. I clap hands by bringing my right palm down to the left. The palms are square, as my clubface should be at impact.

RIGHT HAND ONLY DRILL

Try putting with your right hand only, to get your senses in tune with the putter face and your right hand. Work on trying to get the palm of your right hand to face the target at impact. If your palm is square, the clubface is square.

THREE-TEE BALANCE STROKE DRILL

 This drill continues helping you build a good putting stroke without having to concentrate on distance. I place three tees in the ground using my putter grip as the measure. The center tee is the address and impact position.

ADDRESS   *BACKSWING*   *FOLLOW-THROUGH*

Swing back to match the back tee, then swing forward to match the front tee. You don't want to be either long going back and short coming through, or short going back and long coming through. Both parts of your swing can be trained to match.

PENDULUM SWING DRILL

Ben Crenshaw influenced my views on putting. Once he sets the putter in motion, it's as if it swings itself. That meant to me that on the way down there is no guiding or forced acceleration. You just have to move the putter away from the ball and let it swing freely.

You can develop this pendulum feel by using a whiffle ball tied to the end of a string. Hold the top of the rope on the grip and swing back and forth. If you swing smoothly, as a pendulum, the ball will stay in pace with the shaft.

PENDULUM PACE DRILL

A metronome can help rhythm and pace. After setting the metronome to the tempo best suited to my stroke, I stay in time with the beat it emits, stroking back and forth.

Short Game Problems: Putting Problems

5

TOUR TRAILER CURES

Competing at the highest levels of the sport, today's PGA TOUR and SENIOR PGA TOUR players take meticulous care of their two most important tools of the trade: their bodies and clubs. In the scheme of things clubs are replaced frequently and bodies must be stretched and strengthened daily for maximum performance.

At each tournament the health and equipment trailers are vital to maintaining the finely tuned bodies and clubs of today's outstanding professionals.

You'll find HealthSouth specialist Ralph Simpson waiting to demonstrate some stretches that help the TOUR players raise their performance levels and prevent injuries.

In the SST equipment trailer, you'll learn how they "PURE" a shaft. If you have some clubs in your bag that never have felt quite right and produce shots that vary from your normal patterns, your technique might not be the problem. This is one problem that might be cured just by adjusting the club shaft.

STRETCHES

Consistently hitting good shots requires joint flexibility. Is your instructor asking you to make swing corrections your body can't handle? If an instructor says you'll get used to it, they're wrong. Instructors can correct as they watch, but when you practice alone your body reverts back to the path of least resistance because certain areas are not flexible enough to accept the changes.

The courses may change, but each week players on both the PGA TOUR and SENIOR TOUR count on the 48-foot HealthSouth fitness trailers to be on site. The therapists provide rehabilitative and preventive care for TOUR members.

In this section, therapist Ralph Simpson becomes your specialist as he turns his attention to helping you perform better on the course. These easy stretches only take a few minutes each day but you will feel better and be capable of performing at higher levels.

STRETCHING FOR ROTATION

How important is rotation for a golfer? Since golf is a series of rotations, the turn is all-important to anyone playing the game. The ability to get the shoulders turned back in the backswing, coming down through the ball at impact and turning into the follow-through generates all the clubhead speed.

Consistent golfers need to move freely without any joint stiffness as they rotate back and through the ball. Any blockage or impingement along the way results in swing-altering compensations. The areas of rotation that play important roles in the golf swing are hips, rib cage, shoulder joints, and the joint made by the shoulder blade on the rib cage.

CHAIR ROTATION

This stretch should be done once a day; twice if you are extremely inflexible. I also suggest doing it in your golf cart as one of the primary stretches before hitting balls.

ADDRESS POSITION

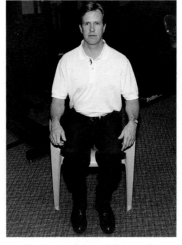

1 Sit up straight with your knees together so the pelvis stays squarely on the chair. Your head stares at a point on the floor where an imaginary ball would be throughout the stretch. As you do this stretch, you will find the twist creates a feeling of resistance similar to what you experience in your golf swing. In both steps 2 and 3 hold for 20 to 40 seconds while you breathe naturally. It's normal to feel a lessening of the tension as you stretch but you should not feel pain at any time.

BACKSWING

2 Rotate slowly back, gripping the chair with both hands. Notice how the shoulders turned under the chin. Never force the movement. Instead, gently stretch your way through it.

FOLLOW-THROUGH

3 Rotate toward the impact area and then follow through, gripping the chair with both hands. You should feel the stretch in the shoulder blades and just below, in the rib cage. Excessively tight? You will feel it on the back side of the reach-across arm. Doing this stretch one time is sufficient.

LYING 90-90 STRETCH

This non-weight-bearing stretch works in conjunction with the chair stretch to loosen up the shoulder muscle groups to make the big turns necessary during the swing.

The hips and the knees are both bent 90 degrees. This stretch is restricted primarily to the torso region, from the pelvis up to the shoulders.

1 Keeping your back on the floor, roll your legs over on the right side. Bring your knees up and hold the top knee with the right hand. The left hand is on your chest. You will feel the stretch from the pelvis to the shoulders.

2 Slowly bring your left arm up and back as you extend the top leg at the knee. This provides a more leveraged stretch through the rib cage and chest as well as the hamstring, calf and buttock muscles, and the deep hip rotators on that side.

3 Repeat this stretch for the other side by rolling your legs over to the left. Hold for 30 or 40 seconds on each side and do once a day slowly or as a pre-round routine to loosen up. If you encounter pain, stop immediately.

STANDING HIP STRETCH

You can do this hip-flexing stretch in your living room or on the range. The increased flexibility allows your torso to make as complete a turn as possible.

The top of the golf swing transition requires your hips to lead the way so they can clear past the impact zone prior to the shoulders, arms and club rocketing through.

As you stretch you should feel left-side firmness and right-side tension to keep a greater separation between your shoulders and hips. This is the exact feeling you want during your swing.

1 Begin with a neutral stance, feet planted shoulder-width apart, just as in the golf swing address.

2 Keeping your shoulders and hips linked, twist gently into the barrier of the first sign of resistance felt in the hip joint. At this point you sag into the hip joint. Be sure your knees are straight, but not locked. Repeat for the opposite side. The resistance will be felt in the front part of your hip joint. Do not stretch beyond the feeling of resistance. Hold for 30 seconds.

SITTING TORSO IMPACT DRILL

We do this stretch with a ball in the HealthSouth trailer because it allows a subtle tipping of the pelvis—something a stationary chair will not allow. You must use a very specific sequence of maneuvers due to the anatomical patterning of the mid-back. This stretch involves moving the spine through the same basic pattern that occurs at impact.

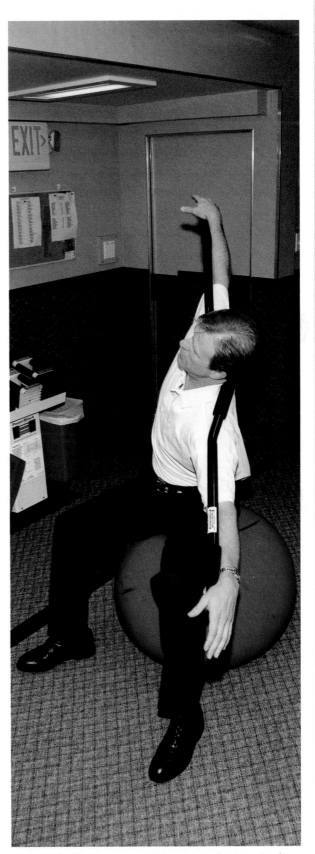

1 I'm doing this with a bar but you can use a broom or a club. The first maneuver is to side bend in one direction until you feel tension.

2 Once that side tension is felt, you gently rotate in the opposite direction, keeping your body in one position until the tension shifts to the next barrier, and then holding that for 30 or 40 seconds. Repeat on the other side.

EQUIPMENT CURES

PURE YOUR SHAFTS

Are there a few clubs in your bag that for some unknown reason you just don't trust? Maybe the feel is different or you can't seem to work the ball with them as you can with other clubs.

The problem could be how the shaft is inserted in the clubhead. No shaft can be built perfectly round, stiff or straight throughout its entire length. Each shaft is like an individual fingerprint with a spine.

How that spine is inserted into the hosel of the clubhead can determine the flight characteristics of the ball. For instance, some clubs may tend to fade the ball while others draw it, depending on where the spine is placed.

Until February 1999 the USGA would not allow any orientation of the golf shaft, but Rule 4-1B was issued to provide relief. Strategic Shaft Technologies, a Texas-based company, is establishing license holders across the country to "pure" your clubs. Here's how the process works, as we take you inside the SST Tour Van during the Buick Classic at Westchester Country Club.

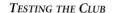

TESTING THE CLUB

An SST technician places the club in the testing equipment. A computer will generate a graph that shows the current shaft spine orientation.

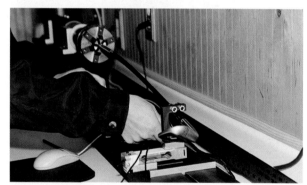

Once the computer is hooked up, pressure is applied to the shaft to simulate the clubface approaching the ball.

BEFORE AND AFTER

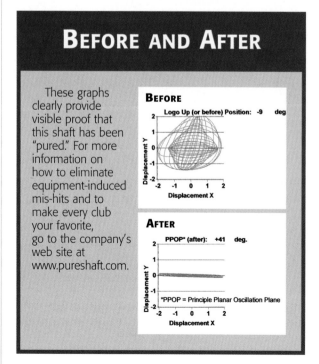

These graphs clearly provide visible proof that this shaft has been "pured." For more information on how to eliminate equipment-induced mis-hits and to make every club your favorite, go to the company's web site at www.pureshaft.com.

BEFORE
Logo Up (or before) Position: -9 deg

AFTER
PPOP* (after): +41 deg.

*PPOP = Principle Planar Oscillation Plane

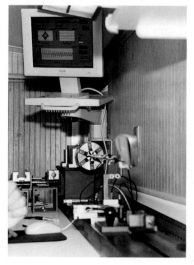

Once released, the tip vibrations calculate the exact position of the spine and the tendency of the club is readily diagnosed. The clubhead is then removed and repositioned to place the spine in a neutral position.

PUTTER HEAD BALANCE

Putters literally come in all shapes and sizes, so how do you determine which putter is right for you? Arnold Palmer has collected over 3,500 putters over the years. While you will never have that many, it's not unusual to constantly check out the latest designs and innovations in search of your perfect match.

The key is to find a putter that not only looks good but that matches your putting style. Should you choose a toe-weighted putter or a face-balanced model?

TOE WEIGHTED

If your stroke resembles Phil Mickelson's or Ben Crenshaw's as you swing the blade open and shut, a toe-weighted model is ideally suited to your style. These two models show different degrees of toe weighting.

You can check how a putter is weighted by horizontally laying the shaft near the head across your hand. Blade putters are most likely toe weighted.

FACE BALANCED

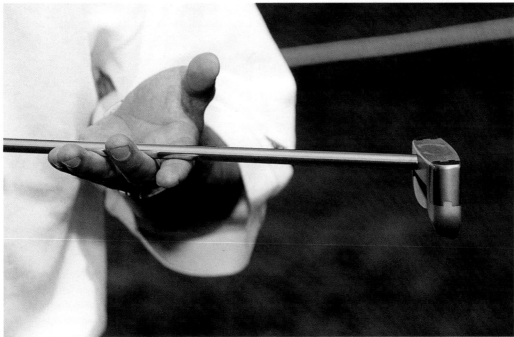

Face-balanced putters help most average golfers. The balanced face keeps the putter square to the target line as it goes back and through.

GLOSSARY

Address Your body position (posture, alignment, ball position) as you set up to the ball.

Addressing the Ball Taking a stance and grounding the club (except in a hazard) before taking a swing.

Approach A shot hit to the green.

Apron Slightly higher grassy area surrounding the putting surface. Also referred to as fringe.

Away A player who is farthest from the hole. This player plays his or her ball first.

Backspin The spin of a golf ball that is the opposite direction of the ball's flight.

Ball Mark The damaged, indented area in the ground caused by the ball when it lands on the green.

Ball Marker Something small to mark the position of your ball on the putting green. You should leave a marker when you remove your ball both to clean it and also to allow your playing partners to have an unobstructed line to the hole. Markers can be purchased and can be attached to your glove. You may also use a coin or similar object.

Birdie One stroke under the designated par of the hole.

Bogey One stroke over the designated par of the hole.

Blade To hit the ball at its center with the bottom edge of your club.

Blocked Shot Hitting a ball on a straight line to the right.

Bump and Run A type of approach shot that lands and then rolls onto the green and toward the hole.

Bunker Also referred to as a sand trap.

Carry How far a ball flies in the air. If a water hazard is in front of you, you have to figure the carry to be sure you've taken enough club.

Casual Water A temporary water accumulation not intended as a hazard. Consult the published *Rules of Golf* for information on the relief you are entitled to.

Chili-Dip Hitting the ground before contacting the ball. The result: weak, popped-up shots also called "fat."

Divot Turf displaced by a player's club when making a swing. Divots must be repaired.

Double Bogey Two strokes over the designated par for a hole.

Draw A shot that curves from right to left for right-handers and the opposite for left-handed golfers.

Drop The act of returning a ball back into play. Consult *The Rules of Golf* for correct information on circumstances where this occurs.

Eagle Two strokes under the designated par for a hole.

Fade A controlled, slight left-to-right ball flight pattern. Also can be called a cut.

Fairway Closely mowed route of play between tee and green.

Fore A warning cry to any person in the way of play or who may be within the flight of your ball.

Green The putting surface.

Gross Score Total number of strokes taken to complete a designated round.

Ground the Club Touching the surface of the ground with the sole of the club at address.

Halved the Hole The phrase used to describe a hole where identical scores were made.

Handicap A deduction from a player's gross score. Handicaps for players are determined by guidelines published by the USGA.

Honor The right to tee off first, earned by scoring the lowest on the previous hole.

Hook A stroke made by a right-handed player that curves the ball to the left of the target. It's just the opposite for left-handers.

Hosel The metal part of the clubhead where the shaft is connected.

Hot A ball that comes off the clubface without backspin and will go farther than normal as a result. If a lie puts grass between the clubface and ball, the grooves can't grip the ball to develop backspin. Understanding this, a golfer knows their ball will come out "hot" and plans for that.

Lateral Hazard A hazard (usually water) that is on the side of a fairway or green. Red stakes are used to mark lateral hazards.

Lie Stationary position of the ball. It is also described as the angle of the shaft in relation to the ground when the club sole rests naturally.

Local Rules Special rules for the course that you are playing.

Loft The amount of angle built into the clubface.

Match Play A format where each hole is a separate contest. The winner is the individual or team that wins more holes than are left to play.

Mulligan A second ball that's hit from the same location. The shot that's tried again. Limited to friendly, noncompetitive rounds.

Net Score Gross score less handicap.

Par The score a golfer should make on a given hole. Determined by factoring in 2 putts plus the number of strokes needed to cover the yardage between the tee and green.

Provisional Ball A second ball hit before a player looks for his or her first ball, which may be out of bounds or lost.

Pull Shot A straight shot in which the flight of the ball is left of the target for right-handers and right of the target for left-handers.

Push Shot A straight shot in which the flight of the ball is right of the target for a right-handed golfer and left of the target for a left-hander.

Rough Areas of longer grass adjacent to the tee, fairway green or hazards.

Shank To hit a shot off the club's hosel.

Slice A stroke made across the ball, creating spin that curves the ball to the right of the intended target for right-handed golfers and to the left of the target for left-handers.

Stance Position of the feet at address.

Stroke Any forward motion of the clubhead made with an intent to strike the ball. The number of strokes taken on each hole are entered for that hole's score.

Stroke Play Competition based on the total number of strokes taken.

Target The spot or area a golfer chooses for the ball to land or roll.

Top To hit the ball above its center.

INDEX